A WHITE HOUSE
Christmas

A WHITE HOUSE
Christmas

ALVIN ROSENBAUM

THE PRESERVATION PRESS

NATIONAL TRUST FOR HISTORIC PRESERVATION

The Preservation Press
National Trust for Historic Preservation
1785 Massachusetts Avenue, N.W.
Washington, D.C. 20036

The National Trust for Historic Preservation in the United States is the only private, nonprofit organization chartered by Congress to encourage public participation in the preservation of sites, buildings, and objects significant in American history and culture. Support is provided by membership dues, endowment funds, contributions, and grants from federal agencies, including the U.S. Department of the Interior, under provisions of the National Historic Preservation Act of 1966. The opinions expressed in this publication do not necessarily reflect the views or policies of the Interior Department. For information about membership, write to Membership at the above address.

Printed in Singapore
96 95 94 93 92   5 4 3 2 1

Library of Congress Cataloging in Publication Data

Rosenbaum, Alvin
    A White House Christmas / Alvin Rosenbaum.
        p.   cm.
    ISBN 0-89133-188-3
    1. White House (Washington, D.C.) 2. Christmas—Washington (D.C.)—
    History. 3. Washington (D.C.)—Social life and customs. 4. Presidents
    United States—History I. Title.
F204.W5R67 1992   91-43807
975.3—dc20

NORTH FRONT OF THE PRESIDENTS HOUSE
Engraved for the National Calendar. 1822

I Pray Heaven to Bestow the Best of Blessings on THIS HOUSE and on All that shall hereafter Inhabit it. May none but Honest and Wise Men ever rule under this Roof.

—John Adams's benediction for the President's House, inscribed on the mantel of the State Dining Room where many Christmas parties are held, was taken from a letter to Abigail, 1800

Contents

Victorian Christmas tree in the White House Blue Room, 1980.

Since 1969 Hans Raffert, now executive chef at the White House, has built elaborate gingerbread houses for display in the State Dining Room. This 1980 concoction was more than 3 feet tall and weighed 45 pounds.

CHRISTMAS 1894.

CAROL SERVICE.

✠

St. John's Church
Sunday School.

✠

St. John's Day, December 27,

Four O'clock P. M.

PRESS OF STORMONT & JACKSON.

The 1987 White House Christmas card depicting the
portrait of Abraham Lincoln in the State Dining
Room.

Preface

————

Celebrations of Christmas at the White House combine grand public gestures and private acts of kindness, dazzling decorations, and brilliant entertainments. The White House was the largest residence built in the United States from the beginning of the 19th century until after the Civil War, a manor in the wilderness for the chief magistrate that served as a setting for the invention of American ceremony, a virtually sacred place that came to symbolize Americans' differences and similarities with mother England.

It is not surprising that the grandest White House entertainments and decorations during the holiday seasons did not necessarily correlate with the best documented or the most popular presidencies. Delightful holiday anecdotes came from administrations as illustrious as that of Theodore Roosevelt and as forgettable as that of Rutherford B. Hayes. Maj. Archibald Butt, social aide to Roosevelt and Taft, observed that he did not "believe in judging people by the way the White House looks ... what a poor showing old Zack Taylor would have made measured by this standard! When he died, the Fillmores had to have the White House disinfected in order to make it habitable, and yet, Taylor stands out to me as one of the great Presidents and Fillmore a

pompous old nonentity." In relating the evolution of family and social life in the White House at Christmas, I have all but ignored most of the important events that shaped the presidency and the nation. Battles with foreign and congressional powers, panics and catastrophes, expansion and isolation, and the interminable issues of trade policy and budget deficits had no place at the Christmas table and are hardly mentioned in this book. Instead, I have focused on those shining moments in the history of the White House when affairs of state gave way to official and private entertaining and the gentle pleasures of family life, including the privileges and responsibilities of residency in the President's House.

The Christmas holidays are the busiest time of the year for first families. From George Washington's presidency through Herbert Hoover's, December was when Congress convened and the social season began, highlighted by a White House reception for the public on New Year's Day. Christmas itself has evolved from an occasion for family and church to include a broad national observance that emphasizes peace, optimism, and charity.

As for families across America, Christmas for a White House family means grown children coming home for the holidays and

Opposite: Charles Kuralt hosts a television special with his colleague Marya McLaughlin, "Christmas at the White House with Julie Nixon Eisenhower," December 12, 1971.

younger children and grandchildren making mischief among the nation's heirlooms. The first family's holiday responsibilities include greeting thousands of guests at an endless series of receptions while out-of-town family members and friends descend on Washington and wait their turn for the president's and the first lady's attentions. Today, for the White House social secretary and usher and their staffs, Christmas means the execution of a plan that is formulated the previous May with the selection of a decorating theme and art for the Christmas card. It culminates in a series of dazzling entertainments and events beginning with the annual presidential awards evening, the Kennedy Center Honors, held during the first weekend in December, and extending through New Year's Day.

Perhaps 100,000 citizens experience Christmas at the White House each year, a spectacle extended to the country by vivid descriptions in the press and media. Dozens of decorated trees and pyramids of poinsettias grace the state rooms and private places of the President's House, creating a fantasy setting for elegant women in formal gowns and distinguished-looking men in black tie who are honored with White House invitations. According to Letitia Baldrige, the Kennedys' social secretary, "The President's House on Pennsylvania Avenue is, after all, the scene of the most important social functions held in the world ... set(ting) the nation's standards of style and talent."

Opposite: The traditions of Americans' celebration of Christmas at home began with an account by American author Washington Irving of holiday feasting and hilarity at Braceridge Hall, a fictional English manor house.

Acknowledgments

A diverse and fascinating range of materials has contributed to these stories of 200 years of White House Christmases. Although the mist of history has cast doubt on some of the tales—flights of fancy by well-meaning romantics—members of many first families have recorded accurate, contemporaneous accounts of their White House experiences in books, journals, and letters. Other works, including Esther Singleton's authoritative *Story of the White House* and William 1's encyclopædic *The President's House*, served as daily guides to the rich and complex history of the White House, while James Barnett's *American Christmas* and Katherine Richards's *How Christmas Came to the Sunday-Schools* provided a foundation for an understanding of the evolution of Christmas customs in America.

I also relied on the generous and enthusiastic assistance of curators, archivists, and librarians in Washington, D.C., and across the country. I wish to thank particularly Katherine Henderson, Division of Political History, National Museum of American History, Smithsonian Institution; Betty Monkman, White House Curator's Office; Gretchen Poston, Washington, Inc.; Leesa Tobin, Gerald R. Ford Library; John Gaz-

zola, The Homestead; Kim Rich, Hallmark Historical Collection; the staff of the Rutherford B. Hayes Presidential Center; Margaret Burri, Historical Society of Washington, D.C.; Frances Turgeon, Kiplinger Foundation; the staffs of the Washingtoniana Collection, Martin Luther King Library, Montgomery County (Maryland) Library Service, and George Washington University Library; Martha Thomas, Benjamin Harrison Memorial Home; David and Julie Eisenhower; the staff of the Herbert Hoover Library; Claudia Anderson, Lyndon Baines Johnson Library; Yvonne Carignan, Lloyd House, Library of Virginia History and Genealogy; Audio-Visual Department, Jimmy Carter Library; Chris Meadows and John Riley, Mount Vernon Ladies' Association of the Union; the staff of President Richard M. Nixon Papers, National Archives and Records Administration; Patricia A. Hoobs, Woodrow Wilson Birthplace; James Rosebush; John Gable, Theodore Roosevelt Association, and Wallace S. Dailey, Theodore Roosevelt Collection, Harvard College Library; the staff of the Harry S Truman Library; SSgt. Russell Girsberger and MGySgt. Frank Byrne, U.S. Marine Band; Cynthia D. Bittinger, The Calvin Coolidge Memorial Foundation; the

Opposite: The Washington, D.C., social season began with the commencement of each Congress in early December, often extending Christmas events from Advent to Twelfth Night.

staff of the Franklin D. Roosevelt Library; Lorraine Mayo, Smithsonian Archives Center; the staff of the Coca-Cola Company Archives; Clement Conger, Department of State Diplomatic Reception Rooms; Bernard Myer and Ruth Corcoran, White House Historical Association; Elise Kirk; Alan Kellock; Keith Stroup; and Arnold and Linda Gordon.

I also wish to thank my editor, Gretchen Smith Mui, designer Michael Endres, and the staff at the National Trust for Historic Preservation, particularly Buckley Jeppson, Janet Walker, and Margaret Gore of The Preservation Press. Finally, I wish to thank my sons, Aaron and Sam, and especially Lydia, my wife, to whom I dedicate this book.

The 36-room White House was the largest residence built in the United States from the beginning of the 19th century until after the Civil War.

From an original Sketch taken on the spot by C.W. Janson, Esq.

The President's House in Washington; (lately taken & destroyed by the British Army)

The Carter family's last White House Christmas tree, 1980.

In 1953 Mamie Eisenhower began to decorate elaborately for Christmas after the White House was newly renovated and when her grandchildren were young.

The 1971 White House Christmas card. Jamie Wyeth recreated an illustration by his grandfather, N. C. Wyeth.

The 1975 White House Christmas card reproduced
Farmyard in Winter by George Henry Durrie, 1858, from
the White House Collection.

The 1976 White House Christmas card reproduced *Going to Church* by George Henry Durrie, 1853, from the White House Collection.

CHAPTER ONE

George and Martha's Twelfth Night

Christmas came modestly to the President's House, arriving first in the giggles of four-year-old Suzanna Boyleston Adams and her playmates on a frigid Christmas Day in 1800. The guests in their carriages bumped across a frozen drive strewn with rubble, passing construction scaffolding and lean-tos still in place against the house. Inside, the children stayed bundled in their coats and gloves as they ate cake and played games. All the fireplaces were stoked, but they provided little warmth, since portions of the roof were still open to the elements. Throughout the 36-room house the walls were still wet in the half that had been plastered. Only one of three staircases had been completed, and the furniture was an incongruous mixture of French, English, and American pieces with peeling gilt and scarred mahogany, hauled from Philadelphia by government workers. The only decoration visible in the house was a full-length Gilbert Stuart portrait of George Washington dressed in black velvet.

President Adams was not a happy man. The mild weather of early December had turned to hail and freezing rain and snow. On December 12 election returns from the previous month finally came in from South Carolina, handing the presidency over to the Republicans, Thomas Jefferson and Aaron

Burr. The stoic Adams and his wife received the first official visitors to the President's House as they also prepared to "retire with dignity," as Abigail confided to a friend.

White House Christmases are a tumble of old and newer traditions, forgotten and remembered customs, a blend of patriotic spirit, religious devotion, and American hospitality. Over its 200-year history the celebration of Christmas has evolved from a strictly private family observance to a grand public celebration with magnificent entertainments and dazzling decorations. Because Christmas Day occurs near the beginning of Washington's winter social cycle, its early religious observances were often obscured by the swirl of satin ball gowns and toasts of roman punch, which began in early December and continued almost without pause until the Lenten season.

In the early years of Washington society the holiday season mixed the formal style of George and Martha Washington with the more egalitarian nature of Thomas Jefferson. For some wealthy Virginia-bred Episcopalians the season stretched from Advent to Twelfth Night, but for many early Washingtonians Christmas Day was merely coincidental with the opening of Congress and the commencement of a new social season along Pennsylvania Avenue.

Although Adams had lost his bid for reelection, he and Abigail, obedient to duty, sent out, by a messenger on horseback, invitations to the first official White House reception.

Opposite: First Lady Martha Washington's holiday receptions were stiff, regal, and essential social engagements for New York City's gentry.

The holiday season in Washington, D.C., which begins during the first week of December, was inaugurated with the summons, contained in Article I, Section 4, Clause 2 of the U. S. Constitution: "The Congress shall assemble at least once in every year, and such Meeting shall be on the first Monday in December."

Christmas at the homes of Adams, Jefferson, Madison, and Monroe was rarely observed with fanfare or particular devotion. For the Washingtons, particularly Martha, Christmas was something more. Married on Twelfth Night, 1759, as Halley's Comet streamed across the sky, George Washington and Martha Custis, the *first* first couple, mixed decorum with charm and even some merriment when they set the standards for the first presidential levees, held in New York during the winter holidays in 1789. They came to their ways with a devotion for the dignity of the office of President of the United States and, perhaps, an appreciation that Christmas was controversial in some parts of their new nation. English Puritans and Anglicans, German Lutherans, the Dutch Reformists, and French Catholics

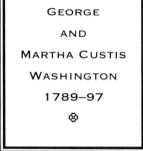

GEORGE
AND
MARTHA CUSTIS
WASHINGTON
1789–97
⊛

each had their own tradition of observance and celebrations. A holiday wayfarer through the colonies in the last half of the 18th century would encounter a different Christmastide table at each night's rest.

During the American Revolution General Washington was always on the move but was joined by Martha every winter, riding in her carriage over cold, rutted roads through dangerous territories to be with her husband for brief visits. The Christmases celebrated during the war years in the countryside outside Cambridge, Newburgh, Trenton, Morristown, Philadelphia, and Valley Forge were each very different from Mount Vernon and Martha's Tidewater Virginia.

On the first Christmas during the war, George and Martha were together in Cambridge, Massachusetts. Martha had planned

In 1776, after the signing of the Unanimous Declaration of the Thirteen United States of America, which authorized Washington and his army to wage war, they travelled to the banks of the Delaware River on Christmas Eve. Martha remained at Mount Vernon as George prepared for a critical assault. "I hope the next Christmas will remain happier than the present," he wrote to Robert Morris on Christmas Day. That night he crossed the Delaware with 2,400 men and 20 pieces of artillery, striking Colonel Rohl's Hessian troops at Trenton by first light. Washington completely surprised and overwhelmed the enemy, taking nearly a thousand prisoners, several cannon, and valuable munitions. The timing of this campaign was crucial and not coincidental to Christmas. It is likely that Washington knew that the Hessians observed German holiday traditions and that they would be liberally imbibing throughout the evening. Indeed, they were sound asleep when Washington reached Trenton. The battle was soon over, and the patriots recrossed the Delaware River before the end of the day on the 26th.

to spend the holidays with her sister in Williamsburg, Virginia, but changed her plans upon receiving a dispatch from her husband to join him. Washington and his army were cold and idle. On Christmas Eve, 1775, he wrote to Rhode Island Governor Nicholas Cook, "Notwithstanding the great pains taken by the Quartermaster General to procure blankets for the army, he finds it impossible to procure a number sufficient. Our soldiers are in great distress; I know of no other way to remedy the evil, than applying to you. Cannot some be got from the different towns? Most houses could spare one; some of them many." The Potomac was blocked with ice and the weather bitterly cold when Martha Washington boarded her coach-in-four at Mount Vernon with her son, John Parke Custis, and his bride, Eleanor Calvert.

At Cambridge the Washingtons settled into comfortable lodgings at Craigie House and planned a party. General Washington wrote letters on Christmas Day. His letter to John Hancock, president of Congress, written on the first day of 1776, observed, "We hoisted the Union Flag in compliment to the United Armies. Raised on prospect hill. Lord Howe, hearing the tremendous shouting, interpreted it as a demonstration of joy over the King's speech, which they had promptly burned." This was the first display of the American flag, consisting of 13 alternating red and white stripes and a field of blue with the crosses of St. George and St. Andrew. A few days later Washington sent another letter to Hancock, remarking, "It is not in the pages of history, perhaps, to furnish a case like ours. To maintain a post, within musket-shot of the enemy, for six months together (without powder), and at the same time to disband one army and recruit another, within the distance of twenty odd British regiments, is

Dr. George Wythe. Before the war the annual Christmas party at Dr. Wythe's house at the College of William and Mary in Williamsburg was not to be missed. In his parlor was a string ensemble, dressed in costume and playing hymns and carols, while guests sipped punch made from a colonial "receipt." The first professor of law in America, he had taught Thomas Jefferson, James Monroe, John Marshall, and Henry Clay. Washington made his headquarters in Wythe's home before the Yorktown siege.

more, probably, than was ever attempted."

As Washington continued to complain in his New Year's appeals, Martha and Eleanor were busy making plans to receive the ladies of the army and of the sympathetic gentry of Cambridge for a simple Twelfth Night party to celebrate Martha's 17th wedding anniversary. Dorothy Dudley, a guest at the event, reported that the "Lady Washington," as she was already called, made a "happy impression" on her guests and was "so well poised that she never challenged criticism, nor called forth the darts of envy."

Probably very little surrounding the Washingtons that Christmas season reminded them of home. Although Christmas traditions in 18th-century Virginia homes were relatively spare, they were virtually nonexistent in colonial New England.

Christmas historians enjoy retelling the story of the ascetic William Bradford and his Puritan brethren in Massachusetts, who strictly forbade the public celebration of Christmas. The first laws in Connecticut prohibited any citizen to "read the Common Prayer, keep Christmas or saint days, make mince pie, dance, play cards or play on any instrument of music except drum, trumpet or Jews harp." The Puritans of Connecticut and Massachusetts were loathe to have fun of any kind. Although Christmas merrymaking and holiday high jinks offended the Puritans as popish, sacrilegious, or even pagan, their main complaint was, undoubtedly, with the Church of England and its royally appointed clergy and officials. Upon the accession of Oliver Cromwell as lord protector in England in

CHRISTMAS AT VALLEY FORGE

During the hard winter of 1777 at Valley Forge, the general and his officers had meat, fowl, and a few vegetables for Christmas dinner, but no bread, tea, or coffee were to be had. Three years later, in 1780, Martha Washington joined her husband and managed to prepare for him and his staff a meal that included beef, mutton, turkey, pies, pudding, apples, and nuts.

One of the earliest Christmas season traditions in colonial Virginia
was the gathering of greens for home and church decorations.

CHRISTMAS AT MOUNT VERNON

While at the time Mount Vernon was not one of the most imposing estates of the area—it was embellished later in the owner's life—it had a superb view of the river, and at Christmas the valley and the distant residences could be seen in a white-clad beauty. Christmas always found George Washington enjoying one of Virginia's favorite holiday occupations—the hunt. For several centuries Virginians have considered this season one of the best times to chase the fox and to track down various kinds of game. During the Christmas period sporting guests arrived at Mount Vernon from Virginia and nearby Maryland on visits "not of days, but weeks," as Washington's grandson wrote. Since the hunt started at daybreak, the planter and his guests had to have breakfast by candlelight.

The holiday sportsmen were up before cock's crow, Washington riding "with ease, elegance and with power." His grandson never forgot him, "always superbly mounted, in true sporting costume, of blue coat, scarlet waistcoat, buckskin breeches, top boots, velvet cap and whip with long thorn." The chase ending, the band would return to the house, and about the table members would talk over the deeds of the leading dog and the best horse. By then Martha had her part of the Christmas ready, and over Mount Vernon there crept evidences of the delights that awaited the guests. Old Virginians say that if you lost all your senses except the sense of smell, you would still be able to tell when Christmas came near. Past and present, Virginia Yuletides descended on waves of a wonderful redolence: a union of the earthy and the exotic, of richly ripe and freshly plucked; of mellowed spirits and sharp spices and crystallized fruits, of nutmeg and steaming mincemeat, of chestnut and oyster dressings, and cakes still warm and puffed from their pans. One man summed it up as "the joyous fumes of Christmas."

—Harnett Kane,
The Southern Christmas Book, 1958

1654, the holdover of Catholic customs in Anglican rituals, particularly the celebration of feast days, was briefly replaced by a strict adherence to Sabbatarian observances. Puritans were Calvinist in theology, believing in predestination and demanding a scriptural warrant for all details of public worship. In particular they did not believe that the Bible sanctioned the organization of churches and the appointment of bishops by the state. As kindred spirits, the new colonists followed the news from England closely. During those awkward years London must have been a strange place to live. "Who would have thought," wrote James Howell in Cromwell's time, "to have seen … the churches shut and the shops opened upon Christmas Day?"

With the restoration of the Establishment and the rule of Charles II and his Tory knights in 1660, Christmas returned to Britain, but it still took many years for the festivities to catch on in New England. In 1681 anti-Christmas laws were finally repealed in Massachusetts, although shops remained opened and churches remained closed on December 25 (unless it happened to be a Sunday). Legislation establishing Christmas as a holiday in Massachusetts was not passed until 1855, and schools remained open on Christmas Day until the late 1880s. The celebration of the 12 days of Christmas before Cromwell's rule became part of the lore and legend of the golden era of Elizabethan England, never quite reaching the same pinnacle of rowdiness and ribald gaiety again. By the time of George I, little of any consequence was written about Christmas in England or its colonies. Nicholas Cresswell, an English traveller

stopping at Leesburg, Virginia, on Wednesday, December 25, 1776, noted in his diary: "Christmas Day, but very little observed in this country, except it is amongst the Dutch."

As Washington fought the enemy and the cold at Valley Forge and through New Jersey and New York during succeeding Christmases, the English and Dutch citizens of Tory New York City were happily celebrating the holidays, including the New Year, with the courts and public offices closed each season for three weeks.

After peace with England was declared in 1783, Congress hosted a grand dinner for 200 that was followed by a magnificent dress ball given by the governor of Maryland for Washington on December 22 in Annapolis. According to one of the guests, "The General danced every set, that all the ladies might have the pleasure of dancing with him, or as it has since been handsomely expressed, *get a touch of him*." Another witness observed that the occasion was "graced by the beauty and the chivalry of the patriotic old colony," presenting a scene "that has never been surpassed even in the gay old town of Anne Arundel."

Arriving at Mount Vernon on Christmas Eve, Washington distributed toys to Martha's grandchildren, Nelly and George, including a whirligig, books, and a fiddle. Home for the holidays had a special meaning to Washington. As was the custom in Virginia, Mount Vernon servants, except for a minimal household staff, were granted several days off and were provided cash and extra rations of food and liquor. For several years following the war Washington enjoyed surveying his lands, hunting, and writing

Romance has always been a part of the Christmas holidays since before George Washington and Mary Custis's betrothal.

letters during Christmas week, entertaining his house guests with wine, eggnog, or perhaps a syllabub, before sitting down to a holiday feast of a huge Christmas pie filled with a variety of fowl and game, served at three o'clock in the afternoon. In 1786 David Humphreys, a friend and aide who missed a visit for the holidays, wrote before Christmas, "Tho I shall not have the felicity of eating Christmas Pies at Mount Vernon,

I hope & trust my former exploits in that way will not be forgotten...." The General replied on the 26th, "Altho' I lament the effect, I am pleased at the cause which has deprived us of the pleasure of your aid in the attack of Christmas pies: we had one yesterday on which all the company, tho' pretty numerous, were hardly able to make an impression ..."

With Washington's uncontested assent

to the presidency in 1789, the scene moved first to New York and then to Philadelphia, where Theophilus Bradbury, a guest at a dinner for members of Congress given by the Washingtons on Christmas Day, 1795, described the occasion to his daughter:

Philadelphia, Sat. Dec. 26, 1795

Last night I had the honor of dining with the President in company with the Vice-President, the Senators, the Delegates of Massachusetts, and some of the members of Congress, about 20 in all.

In the middle of the table was placed a piece of table furniture about six feet long and two feet wide, rounded at the ends. It was gilded wood or polished metal, raised about an inch with a silver rim round it like that round a tea board; in the center was a pedestal of plaster of Paris with images upon it, and on each end figures, male and female of the same. It was very elegant and used for ornament only. The dishes were placed all around, and there was an elegant variety of roast beef, veal, turkeys, ducks, fowls, ham, etc.; puddings, jellies, oranges, apples, nuts, almonds, figs, raisins, and a variety of wines and punch.

We took our leave at six, more than an hour after the candles were introduced. No lady but Mrs. Washington dined with us. We were waited on by four or five servants dressed in livery.

While the new government began to meet, first in New York and then in Philadelphia, Pierre L'Enfant, James Hoban and others began to design the nation's capital. When Washington reviewed architect Hoban's plans for the President's House, he found the residence too plain and small; adding decoration here and there, he also increased its size by at least 20 percent, a full two bays wider. Washington demanded a home worthy of the first gentleman of the land, a place with ample room to entertain foreign dignitaries and distinguished guests. With parlors fully 18 feet high, the President's House equaled many of the finest palaces in Europe and was first among the impressive country houses of Tidewater Virginia at the beginning of the 19th century.

For Hoban the problem was to create a house for a president who would be a head of government as well as a head of state, a place that would serve as both home and office. It was important that it not resemble a palace or function like a statehouse, and in proportion and style it should embrace the character and aspirations of the gentlemen and women who would call it home. The President's House as conceived in 1792 combined a state floor—including an oval room for formal presidential levees and a grand ballroom for large entertainments—with more intimate quarters on the second floor for the president's office and sitting room, a family parlor, and sleeping chambers. The kitchen and servants' quarters were on the ground floor.

At the time of the establishment of Washington, D.C., as the seat of government, keeping Christmas remained controversial within a large number of Protestant denominations, continuing as a cause for debate until well after the Civil War. For the Presbyterians in the Shenandoah Valley, Baptists and Methodists along the Ohio River, Quakers in eastern Pennsylvania, and Congregationalists throughout New England, churches remained dark on Christmas Day. In some instances their adherents accepted Christmas as a secular folk festival rather than a holy day. But the Catholic, Episcopal, and German churches were all open, decked with holly and evergreens,

A GREGORIAN CHRISTMAS

During the Revolution observances of Christmas were still erratic and controversial. According to one Christmas historian, the change in the calendar helped define an American Christmas, a combination of practices from many cultures. The influences of French Huguenots from New Rochelle, Pennsylvania Germans, and Long Island Quakers filtered into New York City, by mid-century the colonies' largest city after Philadelphia. In 1752 England and its colonies replaced the flawed Julian calendar with the Gregorian calendar, 200 years after it was instituted by Pope Gregory. To accommodate the change, 13 days were deleted from December that year, and Christmas was moved from December 25 to exactly one week after December 6, the date that Saint Nicholas Day had been celebrated in previous years. Everyone was confused. Some devout churchgoers wanted to move Christmas services to January 7 (December 25 plus 13 days), while others refused to move the date of Christmas Day. To further confound the issue, the traditional New Year, which had been historically observed in England and much of Europe on March 25 (nine months before Christmas), was moved to January 1, creating a seamless cycle of festivities that finally settled into present practice sometime before 1800.

their congregants rejoicing and singing carols. According to James Barnett's analysis of the American Christmas, Puritan and evangelical opposition to the celebration of Christmas declined as secular interest increased, influenced in part by the doctrine of separation of church and state established by the Constitution in 1791.

As men of fashion, the first presidents did not behave very differently from other gentlemen of extensive experience of the time. They were sober and careful not to offend the delicate balance of interests of their far-flung constituents. Christmas in the early days at the White House was subdued, more a time for family, friends, and worship than part of the Washington social scene. Each December Congress's march down from Capitol Hill to the President's House on Pennsylvania Avenue began the new social season that continued throughout the winter. For the first 100 years a White House Christmas was simply an aside, providing a pause for some peace, comfort, and good cheer within the maelstrom of visiting dignitaries and tedious receiving lines, wars and depressions, trade tariff legislation and lame-duck valedictories.

As the founding fathers forged this new culture, sensibility, and a set of customs for the use of what they called "the American people," they were chiefly working for a population who, in 1800, were largely of British descent. Although they fought the British twice in 20 years, the families of the first presidents were well conditioned to emulate or be envious of the social, religious, and domestic life of the English gentry with their country manors and courtly manners, purebred dogs, mincemeat pies, and Christmas customs. From George Washington at Cambridge to Andrew Jackson at New Orleans, the adversarial relationship between the subjects of George III and the patriots of the New World did not extend to many important parts of private life.

A certain amount of perplexity ensued in the new city in the new nation at the beginning of a new century. For the early presidents and their wives a deep chasm existed between the responsibilities of the British gentry, which were similar to their own, and the unctuous snobbery propounded by British royalty. They held wealth, morals, erudition, intellect, and good manners in high regard while condemning unbridled power, primogenital inheritance, and religious and civic hegemony. The Americans, having developed a distaste for the trappings of royalty, sought leaders of honest behavior and countenance.

Without question most American presidents could claim distinguished, even semiaristocratic origins. George Washington, born to an honorable family of high distinction, was the great-grandson of Col. John Washington, a member of the Virginia House of Burgesses in 1675. John Adams observed that "almost all the business of [his] town was managed" by his father. In marrying Suzanna Boyleston, the elder Adams thus married into one of the leading families of Massachusetts, a partnership that, according to the second president, "lifted the Adams family of Braintree out of the obscurity of small town life." Thomas

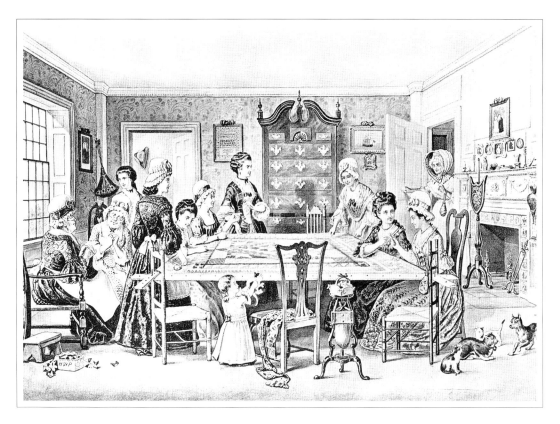

Jefferson's family had been prosperous in Virginia for at least four generations, and his mother, Jane Randolph, hailed from one of the venerable families of Virginia. For several generations the Madison and Monroe families had owned rich land and many slaves and claimed politicians and raconteurs before their ascent to the White House. Of all the presidents of the United States, from George Washington to George Bush, all but five claim ancestry from the British Isles. Of these, 23 have origins in England, four in Scotland, five in Ulster, and two in the Republic of Ireland. The great majority of these British forebears of U.S. presidents arrived early in America: 16 came before 1677, 12 before 1640. The ancesters of only four presidents—Buchanan, Arthur, Wilson, and Kennedy—

arrived after the Declaration of Independence.

With the differences between England and the United States at the vortex of political warfare, it is likely that Jefferson and his friends were bemused by the outward similarities with their opponents, since their houses, fashions, and furnishings looked the same as those of Kent and Somerset. As leaders of American society and as keepers of Christmas in the notch between Anglican Virginia and Catholic Maryland, the early presidents could not escape their roots even as they struggled to establish an identity independent from England. While America fought to establish itself as something new and different, it also depended on England for trade and many of the necessities of the good life.

CHAPTER TWO

A Home for the Holidays

While unconsciously British in taste and self-consciously educated in English ways, the first Virginia presidents, led by Jefferson, were, foremost, the founders of the American Enlightenment, an age of science and rational thinking that de-emphasized the spiritual aspects of religion and the tenents of the Church of England and its Episcopalian successors in America. As they challenged England's religious and secular establishment, they also created a new set of priorities and practices for Americans to follow, including, according to Russell Nye, "a search for the usable past, for memorials, annals, and heroes so central to any national tradition."

Through the lens of English culture they saw two mirrors, one pointed back at themselves dressed as English gentlemen in powdered wigs and silver buckles, the other pointed away at a slant, creating something new and different. As a religious holiday Christmas was then more a day for church and prayer, according to individual practice, rather than a social celebration. Despite its pious associations, the day shared its season with many other social occasions—from the commencement of each Congress to New Year's celebrations and the rest of the whirl of receptions and balls. In this somewhat confusing and ambivalent atmosphere, Christmas in America emerged from the shadows, and White House family Christmases began to take shape in the midst of each holiday season's social events.

In this setting of both competition with London for prestige and a grudging respect for English traditions, Thomas Jefferson, with his hostess, Dolley Madison, the wife of the secretary of state, set about to invent a style and manner for White House entertainments and social discourse. Jefferson came to the presidency as a widower. On New Year's Day, 1772, he had married Martha Skelton, who died at Monticello of complications after the birth of her last child 10 years later.

At the White House Jefferson was adamant that "when brought together in society, all are perfectly equal, whether foreign or domestic, titled or untitled, in or out of office." Jefferson's rules of etiquette included the dictum that "at public ceremonies, to which the government invites

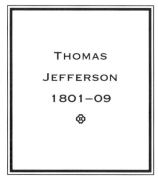

THOMAS JEFFERSON 1801–09

Opposite: The restored White House. After the British destroyed the White House on August 24, 1814, architect James Hoban supervised the restoration. New furniture from France was selected, and the White House reopened on New Year's Day, 1818.

the presence of foreign ministers and their families, a convenient seat or station will be provided for them, with any other strangers invited and the families of the national ministers, each taking place as they arrive and without any precedence."

For George Washington, rules of proper dress and behavior were rigid. Always dressed with the greatest care and formality, he bowed to his guests with one hand behind his back, the other on the hilt of his sword. Citizen Jefferson swung too far in the other direction, installing what he called "pell-mell" etiquette. The response of the diplomatic community ranged from irritation to outrage. Sir Augustus Foster, secretary of the British legation, wrote that

the Diplomats received intolerable treatment at this raw and crude court ... considering the respectability that had surrounded General Washington and the elder Adams, but particularly the former, much was expected in the social assemblies of the first Magistrate of a great and cultivated nation.... [Mr. Jefferson] seemed pleased to mortify men of rank and station, foreign and domestic, unless they paid him servile court, or chimed in with his ideas and general philanthropy.

Complaints from other ministers related to the White House's inhospitable trappings and its "narrow, crowded little rooms," obliging some to "back out" upon their leave, and encountering the president in his office clad in his dressing gown and house slippers.

As an intellectual, Jefferson was sometimes attuned more to the morals of governing than to the details of practical politics. Esther Singleton recounts a story told by one of Jefferson's granddaughters, who recalled the time when she was not allowed

to have "one of those beautiful specimens of Oriental luxury and taste [a fan] brought over by the Tunisian Ambassadors," adding that the affair impressed on her mind her grandfather's "scrupulousness in conforming to the laws in all things, great and small." However strict his manners and morals, Jefferson was lavish with his wine cellar and at dinner, providing guests with the best French cuisine to be had on the Potomac.

The holidays are barely mentioned in Jefferson's Christmas week letters during his presidential years. On Christmas Day, 1762, when he was reading for the law at George Wythe's office in Williamsburg, he half-seriously complained to John Page, who had been his closest friend at William and Mary, "This very day, to others a day of greatest mirth and jollity, sees me overwhelmed with more and greater misfortunes than have befallen a descendant of Adam for these thousand years past.... " Other early Christmas letters were strictly utilitarian, noting the weight of sheet lead per square foot or the proposed strategy for George Rogers Clark's proposed expedition to Detroit in 1780. According to Julian P. Boyd in *The Spirit of Christmas at Monticello*, "Thomas Jefferson seems to have regarded Christmas as a time of reckoning, not as a season for the celebration in the manner which he had been bred."

Other written records suggest some attention by Jefferson to the Christmas season. According to *Thomas Jefferson's Farm Book*, slaves were given time off from work at Christmas, as was the custom on southern plantations. Jefferson also freed the slave Bob Hemmings on Christmas Eve, 1794. Archivists have found Christmas sheet music such as "Deck the Halls" and "While Shepherds Watched Their Flocks by Night" in the Monticello music library. Dawn Woltz, in her article "The Flowers Grown and Shown at Monticello," suggests that "surely Martha Jefferson Randolph [Jefferson's oldest daughter] must have gathered greens from the surrounding woodlands and placed holly and pine in the great hall at Christmastime." James Bear, curator at Monticello, concludes, "The fact that Jefferson was a native Virginian whose family was steeped in traditional yule activities plus the fact that he loved singing, dancing, and children allow us to assume that the Christmas spirit pervaded his Albemarle household in at least one of its many facets."

The social order and customs of official Washington took some time to take shape. Margaret Bayard Smith, a Washington socialite and chronicler, related the round of the season's events to her daughter the day after Christmas, 1802:

We dined twice at the President's, three times at Mr. Pinchon's [French chargé d'affaires in Washington from 1801 to 1805], and they have dined twice here.... I ought to tell you about Mrs. Randolph and Mrs. Epps [two of Jefferson's daughters], who have both been with their father for this past month.... I dined at the P.'s since they have been there and really passed a most delightful day. Before dinner he conversed with me, and after dinner for two hours I had an interesting conversation with Mrs. R.... I could have listened to her for two hours longer, but coffee and the gentlemen entered and we were interrupted....

On Christmas morning, 1803, Jefferson left his office on the second floor of the White House and walked over to the old Marsh market to select the geese for Christ-

Jefferson hosted a Christmas party for his grandchildren in 1805, with Dolley Madison acting as hostess. One hundred children were invited, with entertainment provided by the president and his fiddle.

mas dinner. As something of a gourmet, he liked to pick out a choice fowl or joint when guests were coming to dinner. He was also fond of wine, spending thousands of dollars on the finest French imports for his table. Before dinner that fine day Dolley Madison took Mrs. Randolph's four young daughters on a ride along Old Georgetown Road, purchasing boughs of mistletoe that they hung on the carriage on the return trip. Dinner was held in the State Dining Room that day because the private dining room was too small for all of Jefferson's guests. A convivial president, a striking figure with his long red hair and perfect set of white teeth, was a kind and jovial host, offering food and drink to his guests at every moment. He sat with his two daughters and their husbands, their six children, the Madisons, and perhaps six other guests before an array of dishes, served Virginia style. All the dishes were offered at once, rather than in courses, with the help of perhaps a dozen servants, who carved the geese, passed the wine, and scurried to reheat dishes as they became cold. As the afternoon

Stephen Decatur's mansion on Lafayette Square was built in 1804 by Benjamin Latrobe and immediately became the scene for many elegant gatherings. It is now a property of the National Trust for Historic Preservation.

WASHINGTON NIGHTLIFE

According to Barbara Carson, differing gender-specific rules played an important part in the orchestration of society's events. As was the custom in cities such as Cincinnati and Boston at the time, women were often excluded from evening dinner parties and other nighttime entertainments, but they may have had more freedom and a larger role in the social life of the District of Columbia in its early years than elsewhere in the United States and even in Europe.

A number of circumstances distinguished social life in the nation's capital. Because Congress adjourned at three o'clock, dinner was usually served in late afternoon, typically four o'clock in Jefferson's day, perhaps five o'clock by the 1820s. Because candles were expensive, the guests were often out the door before the hall sconces were lighted. For Washingtonians and White House guests, these distinctions were perhaps less important.

The ruling class of Washington society, apart from a few members of the Virginia and Maryland landed gentry, consisted of foreign diplomats, wealthy visitors from New York, and a select few families of public officials, all revolving around the congressional calendar and the savoir faire of the president and his wife or hostess. In some ways social mores in the city's earliest days were more English or French than American, following the influence of key diplomats on the social affairs and entertainments in official Washington and reflecting the rarified lineage of the first presidents. The "City in the Widerness" received a steady stream of visitors from New York, Philadelphia, and other centers of wealth and sophistication, and for a woman a journey there during the winter social season was something of a lark and an adventure.

Washington had very few complete households, for the majority of men coming to the capital on business did not bring their wives and children with them. Most members of Congress and other temporary residents found food and shelter at a growing number of unimpressive, though expensive, boarding houses. As a consequence, there were fewer gentlewomen in Washington than in other cities, with fewer strictures on their behavior. Considering the egalitarian spirit of Jefferson's drawing room, along with Dolley Madison's feminine influence, women probably enjoyed a wider berth in the social bustle of the White House than in other American places.

daylight dimmed, eight large silver candelabra with dozens of wax candles were lighted to illuminate a feast that ended with specially baked cranberry tarts for the children.

The next day, writing to his third daughter Mary, Jefferson did not mention Christmas dinner, but, referring to the Louisiana Purchase, which had become U.S. territory on December 20, reported: "On new year's day . . . we shall hear of the delivery of New Orleans to us." Family letters survive that include Christmas wishes, but there appears to be little recognition of the holiday at the White House. In a letter to his daughter Martha in the fall of 1804, Jefferson complained of the arrival of a new Congress. "Four weeks tomorrow our winter campaign opens," he wrote. "I dread it on account of the fatigues of the table in such a round of company, which I consider as the most serious trials I undergo."

Dolley Madison's experience as Jefferson's hostess served her well as she and her diminutive husband assumed residency of the President's House in 1809. Madison's two terms were interrupted by the War of 1812, America's "Second War of Independence," creating another crisis of national identity and sending Washington into chaos. During Dolley Madison's tenure in the White House Washington Irving wrote the first complete description of an ideal Christmas, which became the foundation of the traditions of Americans who keep Christmas.

Before 1814 the Washington soirees given by "Queen Dolley" were the ultimate social occasions. Irving arrived at his first holiday party at the White House from his New York home, "emerging from the dirt and darkness … like a vagabond knight-errant … into the blazing splendor of Mrs. Madison's drawing room," finding her to be "a fine, portly, buxom dame, who has a smile and a pleasant word for everyone." After the Treaty of Ghent was signed on Christmas Eve, 1814, ending the hostilities with Great Britain, Irving—lawyer, bon vivant, future diplomat, and friend of several U.S. presidents—sailed for Liverpool to reestablish trade for his brothers' import business.

> JAMES
> AND
> DOLLEY PAYNE
> MADISON
> 1809–17

He had travelled to England once before, in 1805 at age 22, writing to his brother that rather than feeling "bone of their bone and flesh of their flesh, only the negative aspects of the English character— haughtiness, illiberal prejudice, reserve, rudeness, insolence, brutality and knavery—came to mind." At Liverpool, Irving was befriended by Walter Scott, who encouraged him to return to his writing.

By 1818 the family import company firm had gone bankrupt, and Irving took rooms on Edward Street in London, near Regents Park, where he wrote "The Christmas Dinner" and other stories that were collected and published in 1820 as *The Sketch Book of Geoffrey Crayon, Gent.* Irving's Christmas is a universal portrait of the perfect holiday, staged at a Tudor manor house in Yorkshire with fondest memories of the season's spirit, "calling back the children of a family, who have launched forth in life, and wandered widely asunder, once more to assemble about the paternal hearth, that rallying place of the affections, there to grow young and loving again among the endearing mementos of childhood."

Irving's portrait of the trip home for the holidays served as a leitmotif for the lives of

Dolley Madison.

AN IRVING FAMILY CHRISTMAS

Irving's description of Christmas dinner at a great house in the English countryside became a model for Americans at Christmas. Irving served in the American Embassy in London and later became ambassador to Spain, a great friend to several U.S. presidents, and the first secretary of the St. Nicholas Society in New York.

Catching the fantasy of St. Nick while he mangled New York history, Irving would later create in his *Sketch Book* a tableau of the perfect Christmas dinner that served as everyone's model, including Charles Dickens. "Nothing in England exercises a more delightful spell over my imagination than the lingerings of the holiday customs and rural games of former times," wrote Irving, savoring the memory of his father, "a bigoted devotee of the old school, [who] prides himself upon keeping up something of old English hospitality…. He is a strenuous advocate for the revival of the old rural games and holiday observances, and is deeply read in the writers, ancient and modern, who have treated on the subject. Indeed, his favorite range of reading is among the authors that flourished two centuries earlier." A good diplomat, Irving wrote with affection and passion about these endearing moments from Elizabethan England's history and his own day without a trace of denominational rivalry.

Washington Irving

first families in the White House at Christmastime, including the arrival of presidents' sons over the years—George W. and Charles F. Adams, Robert Lincoln, Buck Grant, Birchard Hayes, and Frank and John Roosevelt—all Christmas travellers to Washington from Harvard College. Booth Tarkington in the *Magnificent Ambersons* remembered that

Christmas day is the children's, but the holidays are youth's dancing-time. The holidays belong to the early twenties and the 'teens, home from school and college. These years possess the holidays for a little while, then possess them only in smiling, wistful memories of holly and twinkling lights and dance-music, and charming faces all aglow. It is the liveliest time in life, the happiest of the irresponsible times in life.

On the heels of Jefferson's departure from the White House, Dolley Madison, with architect Benjamin Latrobe, began to decorate the Executive Mansion in earnest, only to see it reduced to cinders a few years later when the British came to town. Even though they set a more regal table than Jefferson, the Madisons suffered many of the same slights from the diplomatic corps, with one minister's wife observing that a dinner she attended was like a "harvest home supper." Dolley defended herself admirably in her reply: "The profusion of my table is the result of the prosperity of my country and I shall continue to prefer Virginia liberality to European elegance."

For the Madisons' Christmas celebration in 1811 family and friends gathered in the State Dining Room at three o'clock. Dolley presided at the end of the long table, with her husband in the middle. Mrs. Madison's two sisters, whom Irving called "the merry wives of Windsor"—Lucy, the widow of George Steptoe Washington (General Washington's nephew), and Anna, the wife of Rep. Richard Cutts of Maine—took places of honor on either side of the president, who was dressed all in black, his hair pulled behind into a queue. Dolley was dressed in a low-cut purple velvet gown that matched her eyes and followed classical Greek lines, gathered beneath her bust rather than at her waist, and was adorned with strings of pearls, baubles, and bracelets, her long black curls wrapped in a magnificent turban. Washington society was represented by Marcia Van Ness, the leader of Washington's landed gentry, whose father, Davy Burns, had formerly owned the land on which the White House was built; his apple orchard had become Lafayette Park. Other guests included Sally Coles, Dolley's cousin, and her friend Maria Mayo, both beautiful young women from Virginia; the distinguished Henry Clay of Kentucky; and Col. James Monroe, Madison's secretary of state, accompanied by his wife, Elizabeth, who sat on Dolley's right. At her left was the celebrated beauty Miss Anne Cartwright from New York and the venerable John Randolph from Roanoke, who wore a light blue silk tail coat with pearl buttons and a shirt collar that reached his ears.

Lying flat along the entire length of the table was a French gilded mirror, purchased by Dolley with government appropriations, that was festooned with banks of hothouse roses and represented an artificial lake, reflecting the candlelight from a forest of candelabras. For every guest there was a waiter, who assisted with helpings in the Virginia style—all courses served at one

Opposite: Dutch settlers during the Christmas season in New Amsterdam. In his tongue-in-cheek *History of New York from the Beginning of the World to the End of the Dutch Dynasty by Deidrich Knickerbocker,* Washington Irving in 1809 introduced Saint Nicholas as the patron saint of the *Goede Vrouw,* the ship that brought the first settlers to New Amsterdam on Christmas Day.

"The White House" as the name of the Executive Mansion came into use about 1820. It was used interchangeably with the "President's House" in the early years and became an official designation, engraved on the president's stationery, during Theodore Roosevelt's administration.

time. Their dinner may have featured canvasback ducks, which could be had for fifty cents apiece at the market, and turkey, which were seventy-five cents each. If a whole roasted hog was served, it could have been obtained for three dollars, the cost of a case of good table wine. After Monroe saluted the ladies with a toast, they withdrew as a great bowl of potent roman punch arrived. After more than several rounds the men joined the ladies in the Oval Room (now the Blue Room) for games, led by the irrepressible Dolley, standing before the mantel and a blazing fire. By 10 o'clock the guests descended downstairs for their wraps and out through what is now the Diplomatic Reception Room, on the south side of the house, into their carriages and across the great mud mire at the gate entrance.

For women of society the rounds of social engagements in holiday Washington seemed never to stop. Margaret Bayard Smith, Josephine Seaton, Mrs. Benjamin Crowninshield, and Louisa Adams all wrote long, gleeful letters to friends and family of the holiday goings-on along Lafayette Square and beyond. On January 2, 1813, Seaton described a grand ball given by Mr. and Mrs. Albert Gallatin:

Ladies of fifty years of age were decked with lace and ribbons, wreaths of roses and gold leaves in their false hair, wreaths of jasmine across their bosom…. Mrs. Monroe paints very much, and has, besides, an appearance of youth which would induce a stranger to suppose her age to be thirty: in lieu of which, she introduces them to her grandchildren…. Mrs. Madison is said to rouge; but not evident to my eyes.

I am sure not ten minutes elapsed without

St. John's Church, on Lafayette Square across from the White House, was designed by the American architect Benjamin Latrobe. On December 17, 1816, it was consecrated by the Episcopal bishop of Maryland at a special service attended by James Madison. A president's pew was set apart and was used by every president (except Andrew Jackson) until Benjamin Harrison. After her return to Washington in 1836, Dolley Madison became a regular attendant at St. John's, where she was baptized, confirmed, and buried.

refreshments being handed. 1st, coffee, tea, all kinds of toasts and warm cakes; 2d, ice-creams; 3d, lemonade, punch, burgundy, claret, curaçao, champagne; 4th, bonbons, cakes of all sorts and sizes; 5th, apples, oranges; 6th, confectionery, denomination divers; 7th, nuts, almonds, raisins; 8th, set supper, composed of tempting solid dishes, meats, pastries garnished with lemon; 9th, drinkables of every species; 10th, boiling chocolate.... On New Year's Day we went to greet Mr. Madison, which ceremony is generally deemed a test of loyalty, and, of course, the terrace was thronged with carriages from 12 to 3 o'clock, with a constant stream of visitors. Daschkoff, the Russian Minister, was there, and Serrurier, the French, both apparently uninteresting men, but most splendid in uniform and equipage. The good wishes for the New Year resounded from all quarters.

After the White House was burned in August, 1814, Dolley Madison never returned to it as first lady. Having lost virtually all her personal possessions in the fire, she found sanctuary in John and Ann Tayloe's small but elegant mansion, the Octagon House, less than two blocks away. More than three years were required to rebuild the White House, and very little entertaining in the already grand tradition of the President's House was attempted in Washington during this interregnum. According to the biographer Virginia Moore, the Madisons were alone for Christmas that miserable year, 1814, receiving word from Canada that Dolley's brother, John Payne, had married a New Yorker, Clara Wilcox. Dolley's son from her previous marriage, Payne Todd,

JAMES
AND
ELIZABETH
KORTRIGHT
MONROE
1817–25
✥

did not make it home for the holidays that year.

Normalcy finally returned with the first glittery season of the Monroes, who rechristened the mansion with pomp on New Year's Day, 1818. *The National Intelligencer* reported on January 2: "The President's House, for the first time since its reædification, was thrown open for the general reception of visitors.... It was gratifying to be able once more to salute the President of the United States with the compliments of the season in his appropriate residence; and the continuance of this truly Republican custom was given, as far as we have heard, very general satisfaction."

James Monroe, as well as his wife Elizabeth, was a sophisticate, having served as Virginia's governor, as a diplomat to France, England, and Spain, and as secretary of war and secretary of state. Monroe was descended from cadets of the great Scottish barony of Munro and was the son of Elizabeth Jones Monroe, a woman of considerable property amassed by her father in King George County, Virginia. Her brother, Judge Joseph Jones, became a second father to Monroe after his own father died when he was 14 and he was sent to The College of William and Mary. Judge Jones was the king's attorney for Virginia and sat in the House of Burgesses in Williamsburg.

Despite Monroe's wealth and solid position within Virginia's aristocracy, the Kortrights of New York were not happy about his engagement to their 17-year-old Elizabeth, the belle of New York's cotillion, who

For Maria Hester Monroe, the stylish second daughter of the fifth first family, it was love at first sight. Samuel Laurence Gouverneur, Maria's first cousin, came to Washington to become junior secretary to the president at the convening of Congress in December 1819. It was said that he whispered "the sweetest story ever told" in Maria's ear during a Christmas party at the White House. Sixteen-year-old Maria and 21-year-old Sam married 10 weeks later in the first wedding to take place in the White House.

Portrait of Louisa Johnson Adams by Charles Robert Leslie, 1816. Louisa Adams was born in England and was completely at ease with Washington ways, often providing a charming alternative to her socially maladroit husband.

was tutored in French and groomed for marriage into a European royal family. As frequent visitors to the courts of Europe, the Kortrights did not consider the 28-year-old lawyer and member of the Virginia Assembly to be equal to the other available suitors. However, the couple were wed at Trinity Church in New York in February 1786. By Christmas their daughter Eliza was born, followed by a son and another daughter.

To Elizabeth Monroe, Washington life paled in comparison with the gold-leaf splendor of Paris and the éclat of London's Grosvenor Square. Her retiring manner, a nagging case of rheumatism, and a strict adherence to European etiquette combined to dampen the spirit of the President's House as the flagship of Washington's social scene. Replacing Dolley's down-home cooking and informal drawing room, Elizabeth Monroe, along with her married daughter Eliza Hay, who was known as "La Belle Americaine" when she lived in Paris, set an elegant table with an enormous gold plateau—a Baroque filigreed centerpiece—and furnished the state rooms with a number of Louis VI pieces said to have been looted from the royal palaces at the outbreak of the French Revolution.

The precedents for social conduct with the president and his wife had evolved over the two decades since the government had moved to Washington, replacing the stiff formality of George and Martha Washington with a less imposing style promoted by Thomas Jefferson and the Madisons. Elizabeth Monroe, more accustomed to the remote hautiness of monarchs, made an attempt to return to a more regal style, losing popularity in the process—she declined to accept invitations from women who visited her at the White House.

For a time members of Washington's social set began to avoid the Monroes' drawing room. John Quincy Adams, the perfectly mannered secretary of state, sought to arbitrate between the women of Washington society, who were accustomed to deference, and the first lady, who would not acquiesce to their demands for respect. The Adams compromise, which was accepted, allowed Mrs. Monroe to return the courtesy of visiting only those women known to her but permitted her to ignore the strangers in her midst.

As a new national spirit rose with the rebuilding of the White House, the rustling of a thousand starched petticoats could be heard more likely at Louisa Adams's ballroom at 14th and F streets than at the White House. Monroe's secretary of state was perhaps the best educated person ever to run for president. As a child, he studied in Paris and Amsterdam and travelled throughout Europe. He graduated from Harvard College after two years of study and then studied law in the offices of Theophilus Parsons in Newburyport, Massachusetts. After service as minister to The Hague, Lisbon, and Berlin and in both the Massachusetts state senate and the U.S. Senate, Adams was appointed Boylston Professor of Rhetoric and Oratory at Harvard.

To launch his campaign for the presidency, John Quincy Adams recruited his opponent, the Tennessee senator and former Indian fighter Andrew Jackson, to be the honored guest at a ball on January 8 to commemorate the ninth anniversary of the Battle of New Orleans. As first lady historian Betty Caroli has observed, Adams usually performed so poorly at social functions that his charming wife Louisa became indispensable in making friends and influencing people. The Adamses' large double house was decorated with tissue paper and evergreens, with assistance from Mary Catherine Hellen, Louisa's orphaned niece. An Adams granddaughter later recalled the second-story ballroom floor as

chalked with spread-eagles, flags and the motto "Welcome to the hero of New Orleans." The pillars were festooned with laurel and wintergreen, while wreathings of evergreens and roses, interspersed with small, variegated lamps, with a lustre in the centre, gave a beautiful effect. Eight pieces of music were performed by a string ensemble. General Jackson, who stood beside Mrs. Adams to receive in the passage between the two houses, looked remarkably well. A semicircle of distinguished persons gathered around Mrs. Adams and the General, and into this choice

| JOHN QUINCY |
| AND |
| LOUISA CATHERINE |
| JOHNSON |
| ADAMS |
| 1825–29 |

New York's A. T. Stewart's Marble Dry-Goods Palace began as a small dry-goods emporium opened by 20-year-old Alexander Turney Stewart in 1823. By 1860 A. T. Stewart's, America's first department store, would stay open at night for the Christmas season, later attracting Mary Lincoln and Julia Grant to New York for their holiday shopping excursions.

KISSING COUSINS

George Washington Adams, the brilliant but troubled oldest son of John and Louisa, would travel from Cambridge, Massachusetts, each Christmas to visit his family in Washington. During one such visit, he fell in love with his first cousin, Mary Catherine Hellen, an orphan who lived with the Adamses at the White House. John Quincy Adams, her uncle, was also her legal guardian. In discussing the match, father and son agreed that a delay of four or five years, until the young Adams's law practice was better developed, would be prudent.

In the meantime George's younger brother John Adams II was struggling with his courses at Harvard, with a standing only midway in his class. His father, a former Harvard professor of rhetoric, wrote, "I could feel nothing but sorrow and shame in your presence," and would not allow his second son to return home for Christmas vacation. As part of the "notoriously rowdy" class of 1823, he was expelled from Harvard just before graduation and became his father's secretary, moving into the White House with the rest of the family. Mary broke her engagement to George, who was back in Cambridge, and married John, a match that caused a serious rift within the family.

group the guests entered two by two and made their bows, there being no handshaking in those days. Louisa recorded in her diary that she had three weeks to prepare for the party, which 800 people attended and which ended after midnight, and observed that she was glad to "have got so well through this business," a sentiment repeated by legions of Washington hostesses ever since.

The relationship between John Quincy Adams and Andrew Jackson is filled with irony. As Adams was in Europe concluding the Treaty of Ghent for the United States on Christmas Eve, 1814, General Jackson was fighting the British on the outskirts of New Orleans, an unnecessary battle since a treaty had been signed, a fact unknown to the participants for another six weeks. In 1824 Jackson and Adams ran against each other. Jackson received the greater number of popular and electoral votes but not enough for a majority. Henry Clay, a third candidate who had received only 32 percent of the vote, cut a deal with Adams, allowing him to become the sixth president. In the 1828 rematch Jackson beat Adams. Thus,

John Quincy and his father were the only two single-term presidents in the first half-century of the republic.

Like his father, John Quincy Adams was scholarly, serious, and at times something of a curmudgeon. According to his diary, he usually worked on Christmas Day. He did acknowledge the holiday the day after the Treaty of Ghent was signed, declaring, "Christmas-day. The day of all others in the year most congenial to proclaiming peace on earth and good will to men."

After moving into the White House as president, a contented Adams settled into a regular routine. A levee on December 9, 1825, drew 72 people, including General Jackson. The Adamses' first White House Christmas brought a number of visitors, including the Tayloes, Senator Buchanan, and a half dozen others.

A week later, on New Year's Eve, Adams recorded in his diary:

The life that I lead is more regular than it has perhaps been at any other period. It is established by custom that the President of the United States goes not abroad into any private companies; and to this usage I conform. I am, therefore, compelled to take my exercise, if at all, in the morning, before breakfast. I rise between five and six—that is, at this time of the year, from an hour and a half to two hours before the sun. I walk by the light of the moon or stars, or none, about four miles, usually returning home in time to see the sun rise from the eastern chamber of the House. I then make my fire, and read three chapters of the Bible…. Read papers till nine. Breakfast, and from ten till five p.m. receive a succession of visitors, sometime without intermission—very seldom with an interval of half an hour—never such as to enable me to undertake any business requiring attention. From five to half-past six we dine; after which I pass about four hours in my chamber alone, writing in this diary or reading papers upon some public business—excepting when occasionally interrupted by a visitor. Between eleven and twelve I retire to bed, to rise again at five or six the next morning.

Despite having an irascible husband, Louisa enjoyed an adoring public among Washington's smart set. She was known to entertain brilliantly, playing the piano and harp for her guests and serving delicious refreshments at her Wednesday evening drawing rooms. The Adams family lifestyle, which followed the lavish style of the Monroes, became the target for Jacksonian barbs, finally leading to an official inquiry into the purchase of a billiard table and charges of other extravagances with public money. Along with his lavish living, Adams was rigidly formal. S. D. Goodrich tells of President-elect Jackson encountering lame-duck President Adams at a White House reception after the 1828 election: "Mr. Adams was by himself. General Jackson had a large handsome lady on his arm. They looked at each other for a moment and then General Jackson moved forward, and reaching out his long arm, said: 'How do you do, Mr. Adams? I give you my left hand, for the right, as you see, is devoted to the fair: I hope you are well, sir.'" A chill descended on the room as Adams and Jackson glared at each other. In that moment a new era of politics and the attendant passions of those who reside in the White House took an abrupt turn, never again to recover quite the same minuet of manners and regal elaborations of Washington's social season. In future administrations entertainments and rituals were often circumscribed by the conscious avoidance of imperial appearance. Soon, Jackson's egalitarianism would popularize the presidency while also restraining the tendency toward excessive pomp in the White House.

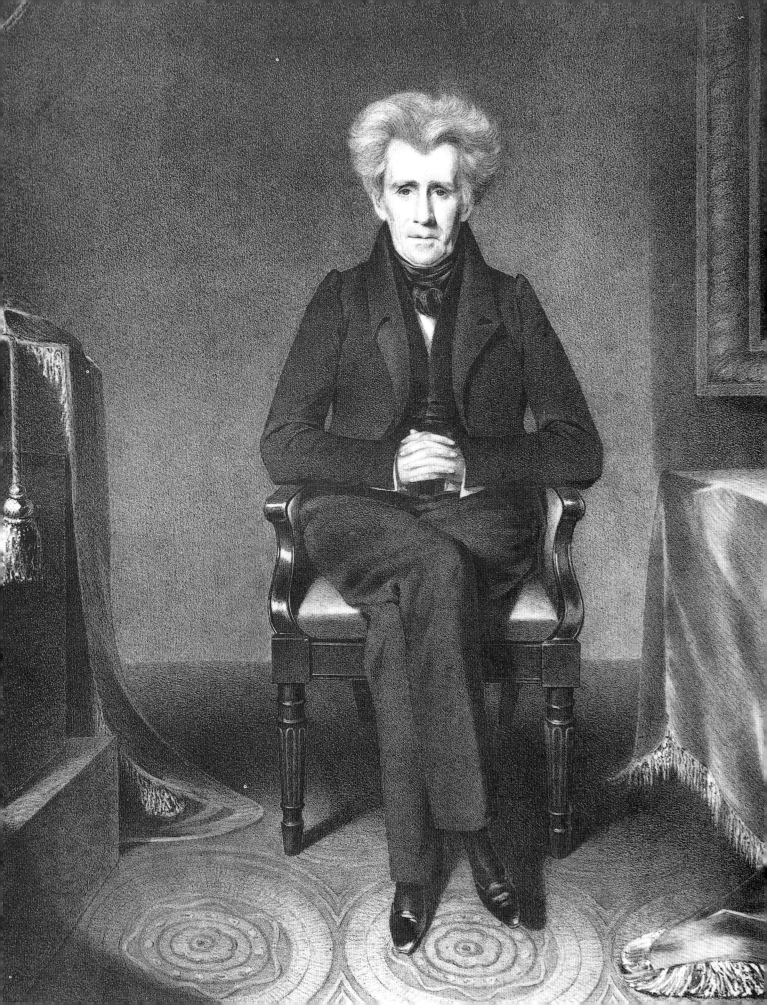

CHAPTER THREE
A People's Christmas

After his election to the presidency in 1828, Andrew Jackson travelled to Nashville to settle his affairs and pick up his wife, Rachel, planning to return in the new year to assume the presidency. While shopping for her inaugural gown, she suffered a heart attack, collapsed, and died a few days later, on December 22. General Jackson buried his wife in her inaugural dress in the garden at the Hermitage on Christmas Eve, 1828. When Jackson left Tennessee, he was accompanied by Rachel's nephew, Andrew Jackson Donelson, and his wife, Emily.

Change came not only to Washington but also to the entire country as civic pride, anti-intellectualism, and home-town boosterism combined to define a new national spirit. Adams was the last of the old guard, declaring, upon his refusal to attend the 1833 Harvard College commencement, at which President Jackson was scheduled to receive an honorary degree, "I would not be present to see my darling Harvard disgrace herself by conferring a Doctor's degree upon a barbarian and savage who can scarcely spell his own name."

Westward expansion and populism had an effect on American culture, and Christmas-keeping traditions also became more democratic. The upper-class, high-church, East Coast establishment was now in competition with places like Charleston, Natchez, Pittsburgh, St. Louis, and Cincinnati in the molding of an American personality. By then Christmas, according to Katherine Richards, "had emerged from its Roman Catholic associations and had been recognized as a part of the general inheritance of Christendom." In an era of frontier sensibility the folk customs of Christmas, quite apart from religious observances, began to take hold as the range of European traditions—German, Dutch, English, and French—commingled to create something new and uniquely American. The various secular associations of Christmas first flowered in the 1830s: store decorations, newspaper advertising of Christmas gifts, the custom of sending Christmas cards and putting up Christmas trees; the use of holly, ivy, and mistletoe in both public and private places, the public recognition of Christmas as a holiday from work, family reunions, Santa Claus's gift-bringing visit, school vacations, caroling, festive foods and drinks,

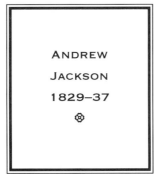

ANDREW
JACKSON
1829–37
✸

Opposite: "Adams can write, Jackson can fight!" was the battle cry of the populists who swept Old Hickory into office. The old aristocracy was replaced by popular democracy. According to Richard Hofstadtler, "In headlong rebellion against the European past, Americans thought of 'decadent' Europe as more barbarous than 'natural' America." Indeed, Jackson had killed both Indians and British soldiers.

Christmas gift-giving customs in Virginia were well ahead of those of New York. By 1840 the *Alexandria Gazette* listed a number of Christmas advertisements and articles, such as this one:

CHRISTMAS TIMES

The undersigned most respectfully presents to his numerous and more especially to his youthful friends the kind compliments of the season; and wishes them all a happy Christmas and a merry New Year. He announces to the public that, in compliance with his long established custom he will have his establishment BRILLIANTLY ILLUMINATED! commencing on Christmas Eve—to-night will be presented A STATUE OF QUEEN VICTORIA, as she is arrayed in her bridal robes. He has also furnished his refectory with a bountiful supply of Cakes, Candies, Confectionery and Nuts together with a beautiful assortment of Toys of all kinds. He indulges and hopes that his young friends will pay him a visit during this season of festivity, bringing with them their Christmas pennies. They will gladly be waited on by their servant, JOHN FRANCIS.

plays, the exchange of gifts by adults (gift giving to children came earlier), and a real or imaginary background of a winter landscape of ice and snow.

The associations between the evolution of American Christmas customs and the development of middle-class domesticity are undoubtedly connected, as prosperity, better homes, decent sanitation, adequate education, good manners, and tolerance began to evolve in the cities and across the prairie. On Main Street the industrial revolution helped create a consumer marketplace; retailers began to recognize the special character of Christmas gift giving as an opportunity to make sales. The first reference to a gift-filled stocking in America appeared in a small anonymous book, *A New Year's Present*, in 1821 in New York. Edward Everett Hale, who was born in Boston in 1822, recalled receiving as a child of three or four his first Christmas gift, a Noah's ark. "It was explained to me," he wrote, " that [the giver of the present] was of a Dutch family and had lived in New York ... and that was the reason why he gave his presents on Christmas Day instead of New Year's." At the time Christmas in New York was a tradition that had evolved from the Dutch Saint Nicholas Eve, while in Boston New Year's Day was a gift-giving, party-making occasion and Christmas was practically ignored. Philip Snyder's exhaustive research of early New York newspapers revealed that the first evidence of Christmas in the stores was as late as the early 1850s, with garlands and wreaths at doorposts and in window displays. During the 1854 season photographer Matthew Brady, from his studio on Broadway, offered miniature photographs

set in lockets, pins, and rings as Christmas presents.

The arrival of the first Christmas trees, a holiday tradition from Germany, was first recorded during the same period. The first church to use a tree as part of its Christmas decoration was the German Moravian church in Bethlehem, Pennsylvania, in 1747, while York, Pennsylvania, claims to have displayed the first American public or community Christmas tree in 1830. Several accounts trace the first home tree to the Reverend Charles Minnigerode, a German immigrant who joined the faculty of the College of William and Mary as a professor of Latin and Greek in about 1840. During the Christmas season of 1842, he put up a Christmas tree for the benefit of the children of Judge Nathaniel Tucker, a law professor. Minnigerode and the Tuckers decorated the tree with nut shells, popcorn, and colored tissue paper, topping it with a handmade golden crown. All the children of Williamsburg came to see the tree, which became an annual tradition in the Tucker residence.

The Christmas tree custom was not observed at the President's House for another 50 years, although specific holiday recipes were used in the president's kitchen from the Washingtons' time on.

America's attitudes toward the nation's capital during the election of 1828 was an assertion of the provident in the midst of the perceived extravagance of the Monroes and Adamses. With the first glimmer of an American consumer culture and its Christmas associations, this restraint was more an affectation than a genuine expression. Indeed, the new voter preference for plain talk and plain food from their presidents was a bit of a sham. While Jackson was in fact a "Westerner" and much less formal, he was certainly no bumpkin.

Jackson's White House, while more egalitarian in the admittance of rough-shod strangers at open house occasions, remained considerably more refined than one would imagine. During Jackson's first term the White House acquired a French chef, running water, and gas lighting. The massive East Room (measuring 80 feet long, 40 feet wide, and 22 feet high) was finally decorated and furnished.

Soon after Jackson's inauguration construction began on the North Portico, which created a porte cochère for carriages and essentially turned the back of the house into the front. In addition, new stables were built, and extensive work was undertaken to expand landscaping projects started during the Adams years, including grading the grounds and planting trees (including the

Jackson magnolias that shade the White House today), roses, tulips, and vegetables and constructing trellises, benches, roadways, a parapet wall with iron railing along Pennsylvania Avenue, and an orangery for growing flowers, fruit, and vegetables through the winter.

According to Mary Emily Donelson Wilcox, Jackson's grandniece, "The White House, always an ideal domestic center, was, during President Jackson's occupancy, the model American home—love, kindness and

During the Jackson years the grounds surrounding the White House were developed to include ornamental plantings, footpaths, and a vegatable garden.

CHRISTMAS TURKEY DINNER

According to Karen Hess, an expert in American culinary history, Mary Randolph, a relative of both Martha Washington and Thomas Jefferson, first offered the suggestion of serving cranberry sauce with turkey, reviving a medieval custom of serving barberries with meat. Randolph's recipes for a Christmas dinner included the following:

To Roast a Turkey

Make the forcemeat thus: take the crumbs of a loaf of bread, a quartet of a pound of beef suet shored fine, a little sausage meat or veal scraped and pounded very fine; nutmeg, pepper, and salt to your taste, mix it lightly with three eggs, stuff the craw with it, spit it, and lay it down a good distance from the fire, which should be clear and brisk, dust and baste it several times with cold lard, it makes the froth stronger than basting it with the

hot out of the dripping pan, and makes the turkey rise better; when it is enough, froth it up as before, dish it and pour on the same gravy as for the boiled turkey, or bread sauce; garnish with lemon and pickles, and serve it up; if it be of a middle size, it will require one hour and a quarter to roast.

To Make Sauce for a Turkey

As you open the oysters, put a pint into a bowl, wash them out of their own liquor, and put them in another bowl; when the liquor has settled, pour it off into a sauce pan, with a little white gravy and a teaspoonful of lemon pickle, thicken it with flour and a good lump of butter, boil it three or four minutes, put in a spoonful of good cream, add the oysters, keep shaking them over the fire till they are quite hot, but don't let them boil, for it will make them hard and appear small.

Reception day at the White House, from *Harper's Weekly*, c. 1830.

charity guarding it like sentries, happiness and contentment overshadowing it like angel wings. Known to the world as the man whose iron will and fierce, ungovernable temper defied opposition and courted antagonism, [Jackson] was the gentlest, tenderest, most patient of men at his own fireside." In a memoir published in 1900 Wilcox recalled Christmas, 1835, 65 years earlier: "an East Room frolic and unforgettable visit by Santa Claus ... the most enjoyable and successful juvenile fête ever given at the National Capital...."

The invitations went out from "the children of President Jackson's family," requesting guests to join them "on Christmas Day, at four o'clock p.m. in a frolic in the East Room, Washington, December 19, 1835." While some details of this White House Christmas ring true, others seem fanciful. According to Wilcox, Dolley Madison arrived with her grandniece, Ada Cutts, along with Mrs. Robert E. Lee with little Custis, various children of diplomats, Marcia Van Ness, and Vice President Van Buren. She continued:

We played "Blind Man's Bluff," "Hide and Seek," and "Puss in the Corner," and several juvenile forfeit games ... the East Room proving an ideal playground, and the players, free and unrestrained as if on a Texas prairie, romping, scampering, shouting, laughing, in all the exuberance of childish merrymaking.

About six o'clock the dining room opened.... The band stationed in the corner struck up the "President's March".... [The Dining Room] was the scene of many historic banquets, commemorating great events and shared by world-wide celebrities [but it] never witnessed one which the decorator's art or the confectioner's skill, achieved greater triumphs—Vivart [the White House's French chef]...received hearty congratulations on all sides. In the center of a maltese-cross-shaped table towered a pyramid of cotton snow-balls, interspersed with colored icicles and surmounted by a gilt game cock, head erect, wings outspread.... At the upright ends of the cross were dishes of frozen marvels, at the top one representing iced fruits—oranges, apples, pears, peaches, grapes; at the bottom one representing iced vegetables—corn, carrots, beans, squashes. At one traverse end was a tiny frost pine tree, beneath which huddled a group of toy animals; at the other a miniature rein-deer stood in a plateau of water in which disported a number of gold fish. There were candles, cakes, confections of every conceivable design; delicious viands, relishes and beverages.

Wilcox claims that after dinner, the pyramid was disassembled and "we were invited to play snow-ball in the East Room, an invitation the more joyfully hailed because the winter having been exceptionally mild we had been debarred our usual snow games." The president and Mrs. Madison looked on as the children pelted each other with imitation snowballs, "creating for some moments in the East Room a scene of an excited snow flurry."

CHAPTER FOUR

An Antebellum Christmas in Washington

The fever of enterprise that spread across the country left little time for leisure pursuits. Francis Grund, a German visitor in the late 1830s, described America as a country in which preachers were better paid than musicians or actors and where men boasted of working 16 hours a day. In Washington, unlike other American cities, Grund was delighted to find "an unusual number of persons perambulating the streets without any apparent occupation...."

Other cities had opera and theater, clubs and elegant saloons. Washington had only Congress and the White House for entertainment. Upon the commencement of Congress during the first week in December, the town's hotels and rooming houses filled with sophisticated visitors from Boston, New York, Philadelphia, and even Baltimore to listen to orations in the Senate and watch the surge and spectacle in the House. According to Grund, "In the absence of theater, the Capitol furnishes a tolerable place of rendezvous, and is on that account frequented during the whole season—from December until April or May—by every lounger in the place, and by every *belle* that wishes to become the fashion."

MARTIN
VAN BUREN
1837–41

Grund observed that the Capitol and the White House were "the only specimens of architecture in the whole town; the rest being mere hovels...." He went on to describe Pennsylvania Avenue as "the only thing that approaches a street in Washington," lined with houses and two good-sized hotels that along with the other hotels in town were "beneath mediocrity." Despite his complaints, this aristocratic holiday visitor to Washington found the cuisine surprisingly good, dining on a canvasback duck for which "the Americans might justly be envied by European princes," served with the usual trimmings of jelly, butter, beets, and pickles along with a small bottle of Napoleon champaign.

The families that followed the Jacksons and Donelsons into the White House before the Civil War kept Christmas as a quiet occasion for church and family. Martin Van Buren, one of three U.S. presidents from New York of Dutch ancestry, was born on Saint Nicholas Eve, 1782, and christened on Christmas Eve the same year at the Dutch Reformed Church in Kinderhook, New York.

Opposite: Portrait of Angelica Van Buren. Widower Martin Van Buren came to Washington with three of his four sons and established his oldest, Abraham, a graduate of West Point, as his secretary. Dolley Madison, who was back in Washington after the death of her husband and now resided across the street on Lafayette Square, introduced her young, charming cousin, Angelica Singleton, to Abraham in the summer of 1838. They were married six months later at the beginning of the social season.

Until the Van Buren administration the White House must have been frigid inside on cold winter days, for only fireplaces were used to heat the high-ceilinged rooms. The first central heating was installed in the White House in 1840 and has been periodically improved and updated since then.

Portrait of President John Tyler by Matthew Brady.

The blue-eyed Angelica Singleton Van Buren, the president's new daughter-in-law, made her debut as White House hostess on January 1, 1839, at the president's New Year's Day levee. Dressed all in white, she wore three ostrich plumes in her hair. Later, she created a fashion craze among Washington's smart set with the introduction of the hoop skirt. Although a political ally and confidant of Jackson, Van Buren was much more of a patrician, and his sons and daughter-in-law were thrilled to be the center of attention.

Van Buren was not reelected for a second term and was succeeded by William Henry Harrison, who ran a "log cabin and hard cider" campaign but actually hailed from a Tidewater mansion and one of the oldest and most distinguished Virginia families. "Tippecanoe" Harrison barely made it through the front door of the White House before expiring of pneumonia. He died only 31 days after taking the oath of office and delivering a 8,555-word speech in the pouring rain without hat or topcoat.

Like future presidents Millard Fillmore, Chester Arthur, and Gerald Ford, John Tyler was not elected to the presidency but, as vice president, assumed the position on Harrison's death. Like the Harrisons, the Tylers were one of the first families of Virginia. John had grown up at Greenway, a large manor house on a 1,200-acre plantation between the James and York rivers.

On the day of Tyler's first New Year's reception at the White House, the novelist

JOHN
TYLER
1841–45
✸

Charles Dickens left London to make his first voyage to America, departing on the *Britannia* from Liverpool on January 4 for lectures and a grand tour of the brave new world. At the Carlton House in New York he spent an enjoyable evening of gin cocktails and witty repartee with Washington Irving, and in Washington, D.C., he visited President Tyler at the White House with a number of gentlemen "mostly with their hats on and hands in their pockets."

He also met with the leaders of the legislature, including then-Congressman John Quincy Adams ("a fine old fellow"), Henry Clay ("perfectly enchanting"), and one unnamed anti-British congressman described as an evil-tempered man looking "as if he had been suckled, Romulus-like, by a wolf." Ben Perley Poore, Washington society's pundit and antiquarian, remarked, "Dickens was made too much of here in Washington and is suffering from the big head." In 1842 Irving was the most famous American writer in England and Dickens the most famous living English writer in America. They met again in Washington at the White House, where a reception was held in their honor, and then a few days later in Baltimore as Irving, now a full-time diplomat, was departing for a posting as U.S. minister to Spain. Once again they regaled each other with stories deep into the night, accompanied this time by Maryland mint juleps "wreathed with flowers."

Letitia Tyler, the president's wife, was partially paralyzed when she entered the White House and died of a stroke the fol-

A birthday party for Mary Tyler, the president's first grandchild, was held during the 1844 Christmas season. The guests included Ada Cutts, Dolley Madison's grandniece. During the Tyler administration, Christmas in Washington was a swirl of parties. No social residence in the city was without a silver bowl of Daniel Webster Punch, made of Medford rum, brandy, champagne, arrack menschino, strong green tea, lemon juice, and sugar. Whatever the concoction, according to Ben Perley Poore, the "bibulous found Washington a rosy place, where jocund mirth and joyful recklessness went arm in arm to flaunt vile melancholy, and kick, with ardent fervor, dull care out the window."

lowing year. She was succeeded as first lady by Julia Gardiner, the daughter of David Gardiner, the wealthy New York senator.

The courtship of Julia Gardiner and the president began at the opening of the social season of 1842, after she had dampened the amorous advances of Rep. Millard Fillmore, who was married, and discouraged marriage entreaties by Sen. James Buchanan, who was old and homely. Washington had become an interesting novelty for cosmopolitan New Yorkers such as the Gardiners of Gardiners Island. According to

Juliana, Julia's mother, "the society [in Washington] is quite provincial, tho' I think it's the best place for young ladies who wish to mingle in the gaieties of the new coast." The Gardiner family was invited to join the Tylers, Col. Thomas Sumter, and a few others for Christmas Eve dinner at the White House. At this intimate gathering 22-year-old Julia found the president's 23-year-old son John Tyler, Jr., "quite handsome and distingué in his person—and ah! how interestingly sentimental was his conversation. He laid quite a siege to my heart." John, Jr.,

The influence of Charles
Dickens and his Christmas
stories on Americans was
enormous. At one time Dickens
was the best-selling author in
the United States. Through his
works he introduced and
popularized the concepts of
charity, humanitarian fairness,
and kindness as important
Christmas themes. *A Christmas
Carol* was written in 1842
during the months following his
American tour. The story
reflected his understanding of
the great American paradox—he
espoused the idea of brotherhood and social redemption
that the country symbolized but
damned the perpetuation of
slavery. "God bless him," wrote
William M. Thackeray. "What
a feeling is this for a writer to be
able to inspire, and what a
reward to reap."

UNDER THE MISTLETOE.

was so enraptured with the lovely Julia that he completely forgot to mention to her that he was a married man, although separated from his wife, Mattie.

Julia's first evening at the White House was followed by a barrage of verses and White House confections from the young Tyler ("I excuse all bad poetry where I am the subject," she remarked). She was amused by the scene, commenting that the Tylers had perhaps 50 country cousins in town for the holidays, stowed in closets or wherever, awaiting New Year's. With both Tylers vying for Julia's affections, another White House invitation to dinner was arranged the following week. Senator Gardiner was seated next to the president, who made special efforts to be flattering.

The Gardiners were again honored with an invitation from the president—this time to attend services on New Year's Day at St. John's Episcopal Church on Lafayette Square. Julia remained in her room with a cold, but the rest of the family attended, although they arrived late. The president rose from his seat, bowed several times, and ushered them into his pew, causing such a stir that he stopped the service. The following day Julia had recovered sufficiently and was escorted by Col. Sumter to the annual New Year's reception at the White House, which was held on January 2 that year because New Year's Day had fallen on Sunday.

The place was packed with well-wishers, and it took more than an hour to get to the head of the receiving line. "He surely will not recognize me…," Julia confided to her father, "I have seen him but once in the evening and then with a different hat." The president not only recognized her but reached over several other visitors to shake her hand, warmly wishing her well.

As the season matured the president assumed his prerogatives and began courting Julia in earnest, leaving John, Jr., far behind. Finally, after the tragic accidental death of Julia's father aboard the presidential yacht, the *Princeton*, and after extensive questioning of the president by Julia's mother regarding his ability to provide properly for his bride, the couple were married at the White House the following year.

A Christmas Carol and other holiday stories in *Martin Chuzzlewit*, *The Pickwick Papers*, and *Boz* quickly became classics, providing a bouquet of word-images of Christmas that bound people together in merriment and good wishes. After the debut of *A Christmas Carol*, Dickens wrote of Christmas to his dear friend Cornelius Felton, a Harvard professor, that "such dinings, such dancings, such conjurings, such blindman's bluffings, such theatre-goings, such kissing out of old years and kissing-in of new ones never took place in these parts before…."

For the deeply religious Sarah Polk there must have been something slightly suspicious about the way that Dickens carried on about Christmas. For her husband, a Democrat from Tennessee, Dickens's message spelled trouble for his slave-holding constituents and their representatives in

---

JAMES KNOX
AND
SARAH CHILDRESS
POLK
1845–49
✿

Charles Dickens. At a banquet in New York in his honor Dickens remarked about his new friend, Washington Irving: "Why, gentlemen, I don't go upstairs to bed two nights out of seven … without taking Washington Irving under my arm. Washington Irving and [his characters] Knickerbocker, Geoffrey Crayon … where can you go that they have not been there before?"

"THE WORLD AND HIS WIFE ... [WERE] THERE."

For the first century and a half of the American presidency, New Year's Day was prominently observed with a reception to which the public was invited. Beginning with the New Year's levees given by George and Martha Washington in New York, the practice continued, interrupted only by war, until 1930, when Herbert Hoover ended the tradition, citing the huge number of visitors and security considerations.

After attending the 1846 New Year's levee, Joanna Rucker wrote to her cousin Bet:

The world and his wife, they say, [were] there. The diplomats came in court dress. At eleven o'clock the rooms were so crowded that I could take notice of their different orders. I know that the British officers had on their red jackets—some of them dressed very handsomely. The brass band was stationed in one of the halls and we were delighted with splendid music at intervals ... never did I see such a number of people in a house or elsewhere ... three cities were here—Alexandria, Georgetown and Washington.

The Polk family's Christmas dinner of 1848 included oyster soup, roast turkey, baked ham, spiced round of beef, carmelized sweet potatoes, celery rice, cranberry sauce, grapefruit salad, plum pudding, fruit cake, charlotte russe, wine jelly, wine, and coffee.

Washington. According to Edgar Johnson, a leading Dickens scholar, the author "was certain that the enjoyment most men are able to feel in the happiness of others can play a larger part than it does in the tenor of their lives. The sense of brotherhood ... can be broadened to a deeper and more active concern for the welfare of all mankind."

Frances Trollope observed that

the churches at Washington are not superb; but the Episcopalian and Catholic were filled with elegantly dressed women. I observed a greater proportion of gentleman at church at Washington than anywhere else.

The Presbyterian ladies go to church three times in a day, but the general appearance of Washington on a Sunday is much less puritanical than that of most other American towns; the people walk about, and there are no chains in the streets, as at Philadelphia, to prevent their riding or driving, if they like it.

As a Presbyterian, Sarah Polk probably did not go to her own church on Christmas but may have attended some other service. According to Presbyterian Church records, "there is no warrant in the Scriptures for the observances of Christmas and Easter as holy

Happy New Year

days, but rather the contrary (see Galatians iv, 9–11; Colossians ii, 16–21), and such observance is contrary to the principles of the Reformed faith, conductive to will-worship, and not in harmony with the simplicity of the Gospel of Jesus Christ." Joanna Rucker, Sarah Polk's niece from Murfreesboro, Tennessee, who was a guest at the Polk's first White House Christmas in 1845, wrote to her cousin Bet back home: "Christmas was a quiet day as everyone goes to church.... I went to the Catholic Chapel [and] was highly entertained with a good sensible sermon and delightful music. There was a great deal of ceremony, burning of candles and incense and a great deal of nonsense to me, but I say, 'everyone to his notion.'"

Unlike his wife, James Polk was not much of a churchgoer. As a dark horse candidate at the Democratic Convention of 1844, Polk was nominated on the ninth ballot, defeating the formidable Henry Clay by the thinnest of margins, in large part because of fellow Tennessean Andrew Jackson's last-minute arm twisting. President Polk received official visitors on Christmas but not on the Sabbath. He also strictly prohibited ardent spirits and dancing at the White House, a definite crimp in the style of social Washington. In his diary Polk recorded a visit by Senator Buchanan on Christmas Day, 1845, to discuss a Supreme Court nomination. The next year, on Friday, December 25, 1846, he wrote, "It being Christmas day, the family attended church. I remained in my office, attended to some business on my table and wrote a rough draft of a message which I have made up my mind to send to Congress...." Although not opposed to work on Christmas, Polk did not engage in business on Sunday. After receiving news that the French minister had called he noted, "As it is contrary to our fixed rule to receive company on the Sabbath, the servant was directed to ask him to excuse us."

President Polk recorded in his diary on January 1, 1849:

Toward the end of [New Year's Day] some gentleman asked me if my arm was not sore, and if I would not suffer from the day's labor. I answered that judging from my experience at similar occasions, I thought not. I told them that I found that there was a great art to shaking hands ... if a man surrendered his arm to be shaken, grip and not be gripped, taking care always to squeeze the hand of his adversary as hard as he squeezed him, that he

Between Christmas Day, 1844, and New Year's Day, 1845, Texas became the 28th state in the Union. The following year the country went to war to defend it against Mexico.

The railroad known as the "eastern cars" first connected Washington to New York, becoming by 1840 a convenient link between the haute monde of New York and the powerful brokers of Washington. Washington banker W. W. Corcoran, a frequenter of the eastern cars, shopped at the Marble Dry-Goods Palace at Chambers Street, the world's first department store, for personal items for his friend, First Lady Sarah Polk.

During the 1852 holidays lame-duck President Fillmore dedicated in Lafayette Park a great bronze equestrian statue of General Andrew Jackson, sculpted by Clark Mills, who had never before seen such a statue. Spectator William Thackeray commented that "the hero was sitting in an impossible attitude, on an impossible horse with an impossible tail." A few weeks later, Thackeray, who had remained in Washington, joined Washington Irving as a guest of First Lady Abigail Fillmore at the Pierce inauguration.

suffered no inconvenience from it. I told them also that I could generally anticipate when I was to have a strong grip, and when I observed a strong man approaching I generally took advantage of him by being a little quicker that he was and thus preventing him from getting a full grip on me.

Although he did not mention it in his diary, January 1, 1849, was James Polk's 25th wedding anniversary. Despite this oversight, the Polks were a close couple. They entertained extensively. "Sahara Sarah," as she was known, permitted only champagne and wine and became a leading figure in the fledgling temperance movement that became increasingly important to Washington politicians. Their party caterer was Auguste Julien, the son of Thomas Jefferson's White House chef.

A wartime president, Polk seemed to work continuously, declaring in his diary that he was "perhaps the hardest working man in America." His troubles were not confined to waging war with Mexico. Just before Christmas, 1848, a bill was introduced in Congress to outlaw slavery in the District of Columbia, which brought to the surface a long-smoldering issue that had been declared off-limits to congressional debate for many years. As Polk noted in his diary:

The agitation of the slavery question is mischievous and wicked, and proceeds from no patriotic motive by its authors. It is a mere political question on which demagogues and ambitious politicians hope to promote their own prospects for political promotion. And this they seem willing to do even at the hazard of disturbing the harmony if not dissolving the Union itself.

Slavery became the pivotal issue of political life in Washington as the contrast between the ideal of an egalitarian America and the shame of slavery in the South became impossible to ignore. For English travellers such as Harriet Martineau and Frances Trollope, America was a land of promise. According to Martineau, "Nothing … struck me so forcibly and so pleasurably as the invariable respect paid to man, as man. Perhaps no Englishman can become fully aware, without going to America, of the atmosphere of insolence in which he dwells." The irony for Dickens, Martineau, Trollope, and other liberal and literate travellers was that while the Jacksonian vision of a society without caste and class was everywhere in evidence, the scourge of slavery destroyed America's purity and diminished its influence on the rest of the world.

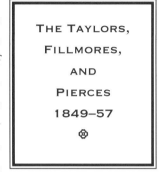

THE TAYLORS,
FILLMORES,
AND
PIERCES
1849–57
✤

During the decade before the Civil War, the city of Washington continued to modernize. In 1848 the Baltimore Gas Company lighted the Capitol and street lights down Pennsylvania Avenue to the White House, providing a safer and more cheerful environ for evening activities. During Gen. Zachary "Rough and Ready" Taylor's brief, subdued term (1849–50), most entertaining was confined

CALLING CARDS IN THE GILDED AGE

According to the social historian Russell Lynes, visitors from places like Cincinnati and St. Louis were "dismayed at how unentertaining the 'entertainments' which took place in the parlor could be." He observed that "the dictates of gentility coupled with a kind of sentimental piety tended to make the parlor and its amusements more and more restrained and constraining." In 1870 Mark Twain lampooned the social pretensions of the use of cards in Washington:

Mrs. A. pays her annual visit, sits in her carriage and sends in her card with the lower right-hand corner turned down, which signifies that she has "called in person"; Mrs. B. sends down word that she is "engaged" or "wishes to be excused"—or if she is a parvenu and low-bred, she perhaps sends word that she is "not at home." Very good; Mrs. A. drives on happy and content. If Mrs. A.'s daughter marries, or a child is born to the family, Mrs. B. calls, sends in a card with the upper left-hand corner turned down, and then goes along about her affairs,—for an inverted corner means "Congrat-ulations." If Mrs. B.'s husband falls downstairs and breaks his neck, Mrs. A calls, leaves her card with the upper right-hand corner turned down and then takes her departure; this corner means "Condolence." It is very necessary to get the corners right, else one may unintentionally condole with a friend on a wedding or congratulate her upon a funeral. If either lady is about to leave the city, she goes to the other's house and leaves her card with "P.P.C." engraved under the name—which signified, "Pay Parting Call" [actually, pour prendre congé (to take leave)].

Margaret Bayard Smith, the early social chronicler, pronounced the customs of calling on women "silly" and complained that her visiting list was one of the smallest of any in Washington, "yet to keep up the interchange with only 70 or 80 persons consumes almost all my morning hours." Presenting this fact to a friend one day, she was shocked to discover that her friend's list contained more than 500 names.

Prince Albert and Queen Victoria were pictured with a Christmas tree at Windsor Castle in a full-page engraving in the *Illustrated London News* in 1848, setting the fashion for ornamented table trees at Christmas in England. The same illustration was copied and published in *Harper's Weekly* at least twice during the 1850s (with the royal likenesses changed, Victoria's coronet removed, and American flags added), implying perhaps that the subjects in the drawing were the Pierces. Dr. John Watkins, a member of the court of Queen Charlotte, wife of George III and Victoria's grandmother , recounted the presence of a Christmas tree in the Queen's Lodge at Windsor as early as Christmas Day, 1800.

to the family circle, which included Sen. Jefferson Davis and his wife, Varina. Davis had first been married to Knox, the Taylors' oldest daughter, who died in Mississippi three months after their wedding. Margaret Smith Taylor, the first lady, smoked a corncob pipe and remained upstairs at the White House with her knitting most of the time.

After one Christmas as president, Taylor died and was suceeded by Vice President Millard Fillmore, who witnessed the spectacular Christmas Eve, 1851, fire at the Library of Congress, which destroyed two-thirds of the collection acquired from Thomas Jefferson. The same year the first cooking stove was installed in the White House; the kitchen staff, who preferred to use a fireplace, quit in protest until an expert from the Patent Office spent a day instructing them in how to regulate the heat with dampers. Abigail Fillmore did not officially entertain too often, preferring the company of New York and London's visiting literati and artists to Washington's diplomats and social cave dwellers.

On the Mall the cornerstone of the Washington Monument was laid in 1848.

In 1853 the orangery at the White House was expanded into a grand greenhouse, and arrangements of cut flowers were in evidence throughout the year. If the capital was becoming more cosmopolitan, fashionable Washingtonians still continued to troop to Manhattan to shop. One new store was Lord and Taylor's emporium at Grand and Christie streets, which boasted a large rotunda, cathedral windows, and wall-to-wall carpeting.

Several accounts of American Christmas traditions mention that the first White House Christmas tree was put up in the Oval Room in 1856, during the administration of Franklin Pierce, when the president entertained a group of Sunday school children from the New York Avenue Presbyterian Church on Christmas Day that year. No evidence can be found that the story is true, however. In light of church practices of the era, it is unlikely that the New York Avenue Presbyterian Church recognized Christmas. Moreover, Christmas was a sad time for the Pierces. All three of their children had died, the last in a terrible train wreck during the Christmas holidays before the Pierce inaugural. According to Iyla Bonnecaze, the curator of the Pierce Manse in Concord, New Hampshire, the Christmas tree tale probably originated with Mary and Susan Pierce, grandnieces of President Pierce, who were fond of repeating the story throughout their lives (they lived into the 1970s). Bonnecaze knew them and claims to have spent the last 30 years unsuccessfully trying to authenticate the story, but "no one in New Hampshire that she knew, including the Pierce girls, had a Christmas tree back then."

The procession from the homespun Taylors to the well-educated Fillmores and the grieving Pierces left a serious vacuum among Washington society, which pined for the savoir faire of a proper White House hostess in her elegant drawing room. In fact, with the exceptions of Sarah Polk, who forbade spirits in the parlor and the Virginia Reel in the East Room, and Julia Tyler, who was first lady for only a single season, there had not been a socially experienced and sophisticated president's wife in the White House since Louisa Catherine Adams had left at the end of the 1820s. With the election of James Buchanan in 1857, gaiety and grander times returned to the White House, organized by the new darling of social Washington, Harriet Lane.

CHAPTER FIVE

A Blue and Gray Christmas

The "Democratic Queen," as Harriet Lane was known, reigned supreme at the White House during James Buchanan's presidency, from 1857 to 1861, the last administration of the southern sympathizers in the antebellum city of Washington. For 20 years or more slavery and its surrogate issue of states' rights had played a pivotal role in shaping alliances and friendships in Washington; eventually, it would rend the capital apart as adherents of each position found the other intolerable. Buchanan was a curious amalgam of southern gentleman and northern statesman. As a congressman from Pennsylvania he campaigned for Andrew Jackson in 1828, receiving the back-handed reward of an appointment as minister to Russia. Despite his reputation as effete, Buchanan went on to become a successful U.S. senator, Polk's secretary of state, and Pierce's envoy to Great Britain. In 1856, after three unsuccessful efforts to become his party's presidential candidate, he finally gained the presidency without any great personal following when the Republican John Frémont and the Whig Millard Fillmore divided the opposition vote. When Polk appointed Buchanan to his cabinet, Jackson protested. "But General," said Polk, "you yourself appointed him minister." To that Jackson replied, "It was as far away as I could send him out of my sight and where he could do the least harm. I would have sent him to the North Pole if we had kept a minister there."

Harriet Lane, Buchanan's ward and niece who had been orphaned at age 10, accompanied her bachelor uncle into the White House. Unlike the previous young chatelaines Emily Donelson and Angelica Van Buren, Harriet had travelled all over the world. Wearing 100 yards of white lace, snow-white ostrich plumes, and a diamond tiara, she had been received by Queen Victoria at Buckingham Palace; because of her popularity with the queen she was accorded the rank of minister's wife. In a letter to her sister, who lived in San Francisco, she described a visit to Victoria and Albert's drawing room: "[I wore] a pink silk petticoat, overskirts of pink tulle, puffed and trimmed with apple blossoms, train of pink silk.... Her Majesty was very gracious to me as also was the Prince." Later, as the White House hostess, she disowned the fashion of "flounces" and layers of petticoats while setting new styles, appearing in décolleté panel dresses and Greek hair styles (that is, braided up and pierced with a golden dagger).

Fashionable southern women once again filled the White House drawing

Opposite: When James Buchanan became president, southern hospitality sounded its last hurrah at the White House before the outbreak of the Civil War.

rooms every week of the season. In the State Dining Room, using sterling flatware from the Monroes and silver serving pieces from the Jackson era, two dozen guests regularly dined at long, sumptuous feasts served on the blue-and-white china acquired by Franklin and Jane Pierce. For the first time the tablecloth was replaced before dessert

A DAY TRIP TO MOUNT VERNON

Although everyone loved Harriet, some loved her more than others. One particular admirer from New York, Augustus Schell, was her escort when the 19-year-old Prince of Wales visited the White House, the first such pilgrimage by an English royal heir. The activities included a day sail to Mount Vernon aboard the *Harriet Lane*, a U.S. Coast Guard cutter named in her honor. Escaping the royal retinue and the scores of other dignitaries, Harriet and Schell strolled along the banks of the Potomac, picking up colored pebbles along the way. Back in Washington, Schell asked for the stones and took them to Tiffany's

in New York, where they were polished and linked together with diamonds into a bracelet, which was presented as a Christmas present to Harriet as a "souvenir of Mount Vernon." Forbidden by the president to accept any gifts, she carried the bracelet in her pocket for days, finally requesting that she be permitted to keep "a few pretty pebbles" given to her by her friend. "Oh, no, Miss Harriet, keep your pebbles," exclaimed Uncle Nunc (as she called her uncle, the president). "You know," Harriet explained later to her uncle, when he admonished her for accepting the gift, "diamonds are pebbles."

was served, and a procession of wines and champagne accompanied each meal, served à la russe by English waiters. During his first season President Buchanan complained to a local liquor merchant about delivering split bottles of champagne. "Pints are very inconvenient in this house," he wrote, "as the article is not used in such small quantities." Dinners were often prepared by Charles Gautier, a premier caterer and chef of his day, whose sweet shop on Pennsylvania Avenue was the best in town.

Despite Harriet's bent toward midcentury modernity, "Uncle Nunc" believed in strict rules of protocol, having learned them the hard way in the courts of St. Petersburg and St. James. Visitors to the president's New Year's Day reception would be admitted according to rank and station, unlike usual past practice, when "all the world and his wife" created a crush at the White House door.

A card listing the social order for January 1, 1858, instructed: "At 11:00 o'clock admit the Vice President (if he should come), The Speaker of the House of Representatives, The Cabinet, The Diplomatic Corps. At 11:15 admit the Supreme Court. At 11:20 admit The Court of Claims, The Circuit Court, The Criminal Court. At 11:30 admit The Officers of the Army, The Officers of the Navy. At 12 admit the Public. At 2 p.m. the reception closes." Members of the House and Senate were admitted with the public, perhaps reflecting the low esteem in which Congress was held at the time. The president and Buck Henry, his nephew and secretary, stood in the Blue Room, where they shook each passing hand as names were whispered to the marshal of

The Lincoln family at the White House, c. 1863. From left: Robert Todd, Mrs. Lincoln, Thomas (Tad), President Lincoln.

the District of Columbia, who announced the introductions. Harriet, who did not shake hands, stood holding a large bouquet of camellias and roses near the window with several of her friends in an informal tableau. The receiving line ended in the East Room. Visitors milled about until the line closed and the president came in to the hall to promenade. When he left, the event was over, and everyone went home.

The hanging of the abolitionist John Brown in December 1859 radically altered the Washington social scene. Abolitionists' attitudes toward southerners became hostile, causing southern members of Congress and Buchanan's cabinet as well as former presidents and their families to adopt a low profile or leave the city. The wealthy banker W. W. Corcoran, a southern sympathizer, left Washington for Paris, where he remained for the next four years.

> ABRAHAM
> AND
> MARY TODD
> LINCOLN
> 1861–65
> ❀

On December 20, 1860, after the election of Abraham Lincoln but before his inauguration, Buchanan received the news at a Christmas dance away from the White House that South Carolina had seceded and the Union was dissolved. An anonymous diarist wrote on December 25, "Another Christmas has come around in the circle of time but it is not a day of rejoicing. Some of the usual ceremonies are going on, but there is a gloom on the thoughts and countenance of all the better portion of our people."

While Buchanan was wealthy, the Lincolns were not, but Mary Lincoln spent money as if she were. In the 19th century, unlike today, presidents and their wives were responsible for paying for their own servants and entertainments out of their $25,000 annual salary (except when foreign dignitaries were invited, in which

case the State Department footed the bill). A Kentuckian with a southern drawl and memories of the overdressed elegance of her stepmother's Lexington parlor, Mary Todd Lincoln came to the White House with aspirations in an age when grand but dowdy Queen Victoria of England and the full-figured Empress Eugénie of France reigned supreme as the social and fashion arbiters of the western world.

Young men in new blue uniforms marched off to war. Lincoln's first White House Christmas was gloomy, a dark, wet day filled with meetings and reports from the front lines at Fort Frederick, Maryland, and Cherry, Virginia. For Mary the war remained in the background as she embarked on her first social season in the White House. After a long seashore vacation in New Jersey and before her first parties, Mary made the second of 11 shopping trips to New York while serving as first lady, purchasing from A. T. Stewart's Marble Dry-Goods Palace carpets and drapery for the East Room. She overspent her budget by thousands of dollars, pleading with the president for additional funds upon her return. Her first reception was given on December 17, 1861, the day on which the Lincolns also celebrated the birthdays of Mary and young Willie, and was followed by a large group for Christmas dinner and a big New Year's Day levee, for which the new carpets were covered to protect them from the sea of office seekers, glad-handers, and hangers-on who crushed their way into the inner sanctum for a glimpse of the president, now not merely the head of his party but also a national hero. The presidency had not been been held in such high regard since Andrew Jackson held the office. The *New York Times* reported the next day: "The striking feature was the great number of uniforms visible—Generals, Colonels, and Majors were as plentiful as blackberries, while Captains and Lieutenants were multitudinous. If our soldiers prove as useful as they are ornamental, nothing more could be desired of them."

Mary Todd Lincoln had become the first president's wife in history to be actively engaged in public activities outside the White House. While keeping her seamstress busy making increasingly elaborate gowns

Lincoln's favorite story about himself involved two Quaker women discussing the war. "I think Jeff Davis will succeed," said the first. "Why do you think so?" asked the second. "Because Davis is a praying man," answered the first. "And so is Mr. Lincoln," said the second. "Yes, my dear," replied the first. "But the Lord will think Abe is joking."

Opposite: Perhaps the most popular portrait of Lincoln during his term was a photograph taken while he read to Tad. The image was widely published in various forms, including this engraving.

FIRST LADIES TAKE SIDES

Families who had lived in the White House before the war split their allegiance, North and South. Angelica Van Buren, who lived in Kinderhook, New York, was sympathetic to southerners and sent gift packages to Confederate prisoners at Elmira. Anna Harrison, a failing octogenarian in Ohio, encouraged her grandson, Benjamin, who was fighting for the Union, while Sarah Polk, at home in Nashville, declared her property "neutral territory" and received visiting generals from both sides during the war. Seventy-one-year-old John Tyler sided with the Confederacy and became a member of its Congress. Jane and Franklin Pierce disagreed, she taking the Union position before dying in 1863. Harriet Lane, then married and ensconced in her new Baltimore home, also sided with the Union.

In 1861, in addition to Mary Lincoln, six former first ladies and White House hostesses and ten future first ladies were living, spanning a collection of memories that began with the birth of Anna Tuthill Harrison in 1775 and extended to the death of Edith Carow Roosevelt in 1948.

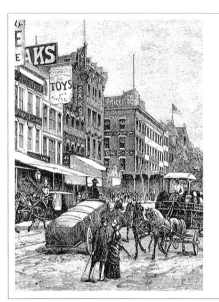

The Stuntz Toy Store, run by Joseph and Appolonia Stuntz, was a favorite haunt for President Lincoln and Tad at Christmas and at other times of the year, and they never left without purchasing several toy soldiers for Tad's collection. They would walk together out the front door of the White House, down Pennsylvania Avenue to New York Avenue, then over three more blocks, where the small store (only 14 feet wide) housed a wide selection of toy soldiers and wood toys made by Stuntz. Noah Brooks wrote that "[Lincoln] would take one of the boys' toys to pieces, find out how it was made, and put it together again … [while Tad] on more than one occasion, had cause to bewail loudly, his father's curiosity." Lincoln was known to have said, "I want to give him all the toys I did not have and all the toys that I would have given the boy that went away."

and driving house stewards and government aids crazy with demands for changes at the White House, the first lady also reviewed troops and toured hospitals regularly. During the first Christmas of the war, she arranged flowers, read books, helped serve meals, talked with the staff, and cared for the wounded at Campbell's and Douglas hospitals. She personally raised a thousand dollars for Christmas dinners and donated a similar amount for oranges and lemons when she heard that there was a threat of scurvy. In addition, all the liquor donated to the White House was given to hospitals for medicinal purposes.

Tad Lincoln, the Lincolns' youngest son, also thought about the soldiers at Christmas. He had visited military camps with his father and had witnessed firsthand the horrors of war. On Christmas Eve, 1863, Tad came into his father's office burdened with books, presents that he had received from the public. He said that he wished to send the books to the soldiers. Lincoln agreed: "Yes, my son, send a big box. Ask mother for plenty of warm things, and tell Daniel to pack in all the good eatables he can, and let him mark the box 'From Tad Lincoln.'"

Tad and Willie Lincoln were the first children in a long time to live in the White House. With the nation's focus on the occupants of the White House and enemy troops only a few miles away, the staff kept close check on the two boys, who rode their ponies on the lawn, played war games, and were generally delighted with the varieties of mischief that could be invented at 1600 Pennsylvania Avenue. The boys were given two goats, Nanny and Nanko. Once they hitched them to a wagon, and Tad, as if riding a team, shouted, "Get out of the way there!" as he rode through the East Room during a tea party for a group of proper Boston ladies.

Tad and Willie were often out of control. They rigged the bell system on the second floor to sound a clamorous, continuous alarm, causing what seemed to be a national emergency among the president's secretaries. Another time, armed with new pocket knives, they carved a war map into the mahogany table in the upstair parlor.

Soon after Christmas, 1861, both Willie and Tad became ill with typhoid fever. Willie languished in bed throughout January while his mother planned a party that would dazzle even her most sophisticated friends. According to her seamstress, Elizabeth Keckley, Mary Lincoln came to her just after Christmas with an idea. "You know the President is expected to give a series of state dinners every winter, and those dinners are costly," she said. "Now I want to avoid this expense; and my idea is, that if I give three large receptions, the state dinners can be scratched from the programme." The president agreed, and a gala "by invitation only" reception was planned for early February. The affair was dazzling, costing perhaps more than all the state dinners combined. During the course of the evening, Mrs. Lincoln, regally dressed in white satin with black flounces, repeatedly went upstairs to look in on her ailing child. Close to midnight a magnificent buffet, catered by Maillard of New York, was served, an hour late because someone had lost the key to the locked State Dining Room door.

A few days later Willie died. The Lincolns were devastated. Soon afterward Mary brought down a spiritualist from New York to conduct séances at the White House in an effort to make contact with Willie. The president and Tad found other ways to assuage their grief.

The next Christmas Tad's Aunt Emilie, Mrs. Lincoln's sister, and her young daughter Katherine from Kentucky paid a surprise visit. As Ruth Randall, author of *Lincoln's Sons* told it, the children were sitting on the floor before a fire, with Tad showing his cousin an album of family photographs. Coming to the page with a picture of his father, he pointed and said, "This is the president." The little girl shook her head and set him straight. "No, that is not the president, Mr. Davis is the president." Indignant, Tad rose to defend his president. Then Katherine rose to defend her president. At this moment of diplomatic impasse Lincoln came to the rescue. "Well, Tad, you know who is your President, and I am your little cousin's Uncle Lincoln." Katherine and her mother left in mid-December with a special pass from the president to ensure their safe passage through Union territory.

During the same holiday a friend of the Lincolns sent a big live turkey for their Christmas dinner. Tad found the turkey in a pen, named it Jack, and made it a pet, teaching it to follow behind him. Just before Christmas Tad came flying into his father's office, interrupting a meeting with a cabinet member and crying that Jack was going to be killed for Christmas dinner. "But Tad," said the president, "Jack was sent here to be killed and eaten for this very Christmas." Tad could not hold back the tears: "I can't help it. He's a good turkey, and I don't want him killed." Lincoln took a card from his desk and prepared a formal Christmas presidential pardon for Jack. From that time onward Jack became a regular member of the White House menagerie.

Like many state governors, Lincoln often reserved his power to grant presidential pardons for the holiday season. On another Christmas the Sanitary Commission of New York sent Tad a toy soldier dressed in the uniform of his favorite

Arlington House. During the war years Christmas for southerners was miserable. The hope of a short war and of returning home by the first Christmas began to fade by that fall. Jefferson and Varina Davis lived in Richmond, a city that by the end of the war was under siege, without enough food, clean water, or fuel to sustain even the president's staff. General Robert E. Lee's house overlooking Washington had been overrun since the beginning of the war. An 1851 Christmas letter that Lee wrote to his son, George Washington Custis Lee (named for his grandfather, George Washington's adopted son), a West Point cadet, survives:

The Children were delighted in getting back & passed the evening in devising pleasures for the morrow. They were upon us before day Xmas morning to overhaul their stockings…. Mother, Rooney and I went to Church. Rooney and the twins skated back in the [C&O] Canal [which had a Virginia side in those days].… I need not describe to you our circumstances. You have witnessed them so often, not the turkey, old ham, plum pudding, mince pies, etc. at dinner. I hope that you will enjoy them again or some equally as good…. The family have retired but I should be charged with much love from every individual were they aware of my writing so I will give it without bidding.… I remain as ever your devoted father. RE Lee.

Zouave guards, which Tad also named Jack, after his turkey. He delighted in frequently court-martialing the hapless character, pronouncing a sentence of death by a firing squad at sunrise, then immediately enacting the execution with his toy cannon. According to Ruth Randall, "the soldier would then be buried inappropriately with full military honors…" among the White House rosebushes. Tad and his friends were found in the garden, playing the "excruciating 'dead march' [with] a broken-down fiddle, a dented horn, paper over a comb, and Tad's drum." The gardener, wishing to have his rosebushes left alone, suggested that Jack be given a pardon. Tad agreed, and the boys trooped into the house and clamored up to the President's office, undeterred by a phalanx of presidential aides.

The president, interrupting affairs of state, decided to hear Tad out. Randall continues: "Tad delivered his argument in a rush of words: almost every day they try Jack for being a spy or deserter or something and they shot him and buried him and Julia [Taft, the older sister of one of Tad's friends] said that it spoiled his clothes and Major Watt [the gardner] said it dug up his roses so they thought they would get Pa to fix up a pardon." Judgment came swift. Tad had made his case. "It was a good law that no man shall twice be put in jeopardy of his life for the same offense, " said Lincoln. "Since Jack has been shot and buried a dozen times, he is entitled to a pardon." With that, the president took an official-looking document out of his desk and wrote with a flourish, "The Doll Jack is pardoned by order of the President, A. Lincoln."

The more memorable date for the nation during the Civil War years was January 1, 1863, when the Emancipation Proclamation became law, freeing all the slaves in the Confederacy. From 9 until 11 o'clock Lincoln had stood in the center of the Blue Room next to a white marble table (all the other furniture had been moved into the Red and Green rooms), shaking hands with thousands of New Year well-wishers. He then went to his office to await the arrival of the document for signing. Finally, the engrossed parchment arrived with Secretary Seward. Lincoln commented, "I never in my life felt more certain that I was doing right, than I do in signing this paper. But I have been receiving calls and shaking hands since nine o'clock this morning, till my arm is stiff and numb. Now this signature is one that will be closely examined. If they find my hand trembled they will say, 'he had some complications.' But anyway, it is going to be done."

In November 1864 Lincoln was reelected to the presidency. On Election Day soldiers lined up to vote at a polling place set up at the White House. Tad ran into his father's office and dragged him to the window, where they watched Jack, the Christmas turkey, strut among the voters, taking in the scene. "Does he vote?" Lincoln asked with a grin. "No, he is not of age," replied Tad, not missing a beat. By Christmas the outlook from the front was much better. A telegram from Sherman, marching through Georgia, arrived with this message: "I beg to present you as a Christmas gift the city of Savannah with 150 heavy guns and plenty of ammunition, and also about 25,000 bales of cotton."

CHAPTER SIX

Deck the Halls

One hundred and twelve days after Sherman's Christmas in Savannah, Lincoln was dead. Following the president's assassination and the first lady's terrible and confused departure from the White House, Eliza Johnson, the wife of the new president, moved in, took out her knitting, and was hardly heard from again for the next four years. She emerged officially only twice, once to participate in a "Juvenile Soirée" on December 29, 1868, President Andrew Johnson's 60th birthday. The party was given by the "Children of the President's Family," who were, presumably, the grandchildren, since all the Johnson children were adults. The invitations, sent to 500 people, presented an elaborate program of 15 dances. Guests filled their cards and glided across the East Room to a waltz and such Victorian dances as the esmeralda, the varsovienne, the basket quadrille, and the quadrille sociable.

Social discourse returned to the President's House with the installation of Ulysses, Julia, and Nellie Grant. According to Col. W. H. Crook, who began his White House career as Lincoln's bodyguard, "the

---

ULYSSES S. AND JULIA DENT GRANT 1869–77

❀

---

contrast between this gay, light-hearted, happy arrival [of the Grants] and the lonely coming of President Johnson's ... was almost painful." The postwar economic boon continued until the fall of 1873, and the nation as the whole and the White House as a microcosm began to undergo enormous change. Women arrived at social functions in Paris frocks, and men discussed their business interests across the oceans, for the transcontinental rail service and the opening of the Suez Canal had made the world smaller. Hotels and restaurants in Washington sprouted like mushrooms, and stores catering to the carriage trade began to trumpet Christmas as the ultimate opportunity to find delightful toys and candies, the latest fashion, and the most stylish accessories.

The Grants had come a long way. Only a few years earlier, living in Hardscrabble, Missouri, Captain Grant had to pawn his pocket watch to buy Christmas presents for his family. As a conquering hero, his world now included fast horses, beautiful women, billiards, and vintage port, and his wife basked in his reflected glory. Julia Dent Grant, beribboned, bejewelled, beaded, tucked, and laced, stood among the potted

Opposite: A hallmark of the Gilded Age was a new spirit during the holidays, when fun and gifts for children on Christmas morning became a cherished tradition.

The Grant family, c. 1870. From left: President Grant, Jesse, Buck, Frederick, Ellen ("Nellie"), and Mrs. Grant.

Dinners at the Grant White House were elaborate, consisting of as many as 29 courses and lasting two to three hours. Roman punch was served at the end of the roast course as a refresher.

U.S. Grant's Roman Punch
1 quart lemonade
1 bottle champagne
⅔ cup rum

Julia Grant's Roman Punch
1 quart lemonade
1 bottle champagne
⅓ cup Cointreau

palms and watched the pirouette of Washington society's matrons. Now, at the beginning of America's Gilded Age, men and women of society had become more mannered and self-conscious, as ancient customs of decorum and politeness were raised now to a fine art of pretension.

Washington, in center strut after the acceptance of Lee's surrender, began to unfold its peacock plumes to the rest of the world. As the American democratic experiment entered its second century, royal families, both ancient and modern, still held power over nine-tenths of the world's population. Into this fray of highfalutin entertaining the Grants marched gamely. In December 1874 they entertained the first foreign head of state in White House history, the king of Hawaii, and his royal entourage. The *Evening Star* reported:

Our royal visitor, David Kalakaua, King of the Sandwich Islands found the change from his own sunny and genial clime into the more austere atmosphere of the west rather trying on his constitution, and the milder air in Washington has not yet

worked a change. He has for some days past, in fact from the time he left the Pacific Coast, been suffering from a severe cold, which made him so hoarse he could hardly speak and depressed him very much.

This visit had been prompted by an earlier visit by Queen Emma, widow of Kamehameha IV, during the Johnson administration, when she made a trip around the world.

A few days later the king had recovered sufficiently to attend a performance at the Ford's Theatre with the Grants and to be entertained the next evening, December 22, at the first dinner held for a foreign head of state at the White House, described as "brilliant beyond all precedent" in the next day's *Evening Star:*

Down the center of the [dinner] table was a horizontal mirror, whose gilt frame and arches afford a fine support for delicate vines and garlands. In the center of the mirror was an immense epergne of gilt, whose many bowls and branches were filled with flowers and bon-bons.... There were plates for thirty persons. At each plate there were glasses for sherry, claret, champagne and a goblet of water ... the china [was] pink and white.... the Marine Band gave their fine music at intervals during the dinner and evening.

As King Kalakaua dined, his cupbearer and two princelings stood behind him wearing what was described as "ladies bertha capes." Every bit of food from the banquet was scrutinized by the cupbearer. Although it was almost Christmas Eve, it is unlikely that any holiday music was played. The guests used sterling and vermeil flatware, engraved with "President's House," and a new 587-piece Limoges china service. Distant strains of popular martial music could be heard from the Marine Band, which was assembled at a safe distance in the hall. According to a popular pianist of the time, Louis Gottschalk, Grant knew only two tunes: "One is 'Yankee Doodle Dandy,' and the other isn't." A few days later, on New Year's Day, the Grants announced the engagement of their daughter, Nellie, to Algernon Satoris, a British diplomat and international bon vivant. They were married at the White House the following June.

RUTHERFORD B. AND LUCY WEBB HAYES 1877–81

✶

After considering and rejecting a third term as president, Grant and his wife departed for a trip around the world. Lucy Webb Hayes and her controversial millionaire husband, Rutherford B. Hayes, settled down for a pleasant stay in the White House, returning to Ohio four years later with the feeling that, as Hayes expressed it, "nobody ever left the Presidency with less regret, less disappointment, fewer heartburnings, or more general content with the result of his term (in his own heart, I mean), than I do." Hayes has been considered by many as someone who "stole" the presidency from Samuel Tilden. One newspaper editor declared in 1877: "This will be the first time a usurper has celebrated Christmas in the White House. But Santa Claus descends the chimney alike on the just and the unjust."

Mrs. Hayes was dubbed "Lemonade Lucy" because as a temperance advocate she banned ardent spirits in the White House. According to Hayes's secretary of state Hamilton Fish, "water flowed like wine" at the president's receptions, although a certain steward was known to dispense St. Croix rum concealed inside oranges at White House events when the Hayeses were not looking. The Women's Christian Temperance Union, just being organized in Cleveland, found in Lucy their champion. While certainly no prude, Mrs. Hayes made her husband promise to maintain a dry presidency. A sign posted on a saloon as one approached the White House read "Last Chance" and on the opposite side, as one left the White House, "First Chance."

In spite of her strident prohibitionist stand and devotional fervor, Lucy Hayes was a delightful, fun-loving hostess who enjoyed both a close family life and a wide circle of good friends. Free of the social insecurities that plagued Mary Lincoln and Julia Grant, she was unpretentious and practical and was delighted with her White House accommodations. Instead of sinking public funds into redecoration (as the Lincolns, Johnsons, and Grants had done), she spent a large part of the White House con-

gressional appropriation on a 1,000-piece dinner service depicting the flora and fauna of the United States. Each piece of this set of Limoges china, created by Theodore R. Davis of New Jersey, was individually painted in watercolors. Archibald Butt, chief social aide to presidents Theodore Roosevelt and William Howard Taft, declared that the Hayes china was "the ugliest thing that I have ever seen!"

The highlight of the Hayeses' first holiday season in the White House was the celebration of their silver wedding anniversary, including a lavish reenactment of their 1852 wedding ceremony, held in the Blue Room, and a sumptuous dinner held in the Family Dining Room. The festivities began on Sunday, December 30, and were followed by a New Year's Eve party and a big reception on New Year's Day. The assembled guests included friends who had attended their wedding and had come by train from Cincinnati, including the Reverend Lorenzo Dow McCabe, who had performed the original ceremony.

A notable detail from the hundreds of thousands of words filed by journalists who covered the Hayeses' anniversary reception was one newspaper's description of "the splendid Christmas plant in full bloom, displaying its scarlet wealth of coloring in almost every corner." This is, perhaps, the first description of a specific decoration for Christmas in the White House.

Fanny and Scott, the Hayeses' two younger children, delighted in their White House Christmases. The president's diary entry for December 25, 1880, relates:

As usual, the gifts were collected in one room (in this case the red chamber) and the children, ser-

Sketch for a portrait of Lucy Webb Hayes by Daniel Huntington, dated December 21, 1880. The painting itself was donated by the Women's Christian Temperance Union to the White House, where it hangs today. With the gift came a silk banner bearing the inscription "She hath done what she could."

SILVER BELLS AT THE WHITE HOUSE

Title page for the Hayeses' silver wedding anniversary events from the "Record of the social events at the Executive Mansion during the administration of President Hayes." This extraordinary calligraphy was created by O. L. Pruden, assistant secretary to the president. To greet her guests Lucy Hayes wore her 1852 white brocade wedding dress, holding her breath as she made her rounds. She then quickly changed into something more comfortable for the rest of the evening.

Present at the 25th anniversary festivities were Cincinnati bluestocking Harriet Herron and her

husband John, friends of the Hayeses who arrived with their six-week-old daughter, who was named for Lucy Hayes. Little Lucy's older sister, who would spend the next Christmas at the White House with the Hayes family, was 17-year-old debutante Helen ("Nellie") Herron, who vowed that she would return one day as first lady. Nellie Herron later married William Howard Taft and eventually fulfilled her schoolgirl ambition. Another visitor was Mary Harrison, daughter of Gen. Benjamin Harrison, who also would become a White House hostess.

vants, and friends in another (the library), and on the ringing of the bell at the door Scott and Fanny ran and brought a single article well concealed by wrappings to me. After some delays and guesses it is found whose gift it is. All got something, Scott and Fanny many things. All at least a five-dollar gold piece.

Lucy Hayes was a popular first lady, drawing favorable comments for her intellect (she was the first wife of a president to graduate from college), quick wit, charm, and generosity. Along with her predecessor, Julia

Grant, and her successor, Lucretia Garfield, she had endured the rigors of life as the wife of a Union officer during the Civil War. Perhaps of greater importance was the age in which she lived in the White House, the years of Susan B. Anthony, Elizabeth Cady Stanton, the National Women's Suffrage Association, and their national crusade demanding equal rights for women.

The tide was beginning to turn on ladies who lunched and worried endlessly about the

"Christmas" Doll House. Madison Magruder, a local carpenter living on 15th Street, was hired to build a doll house for Fanny Hayes, age 10, which she received as a present for her first White House Christmas in 1877.

Chester A. Arthur assumed the presidency upon the assassination of James Garfield only a few months after the inauguration.

finer points of etiquette. The burden of cabinet wives, for instance, receiving New Year's callers, had become overwhelming. The rules for receiving visitors began to bend to accommodate the practical problems of dealing with hundreds of callers, many of whom had dipped into too many punch bowls, arriving en masse on the doorstep. During the Grant administration, a list was published on the front page of the *Evening Star* during Christmas week giving the name and address of all cabinet and subcabinet members, diplomats, senior military officers, senators, and member of society—with a notation as to whether or not they were receiving. For those not receiving, an explanation was usually provided. Ten years later the presumption of every house being open to callers on New Year's Day was fading, although the ceremonies attendant to the White House reception remained fixed for another 50 years.

In the 1880s home celebrations of Christmas throughout America and at the White House became more commonplace and more secular as cities grew, European immigrants increased, advertising and retailing became ubiquitous, and a greater awareness of regional customs (because of better transportation and communications) merged into a new national spirit. An item appearing in the *Evening Star* on Christmas Eve, 1887, reported that when a Mrs. Brown entertained her dancing class at her F Street residence, "the novel feature of the evening was a Christmas tree from which Santa Claus, Mr. Saloncon, of the French legation, distributed gifts to those present. "

The American people probably had not considered Arthur's credentials for the presidency when he was selected to serve as vice president for reformer James Garfield in 1881. In fact, when Garfield died from an assassin's bullet a few months into his term, an acquaintance exclaimed, "Chet Arthur, President of the United States! Good God!" Arthur, a widower, was in no hurry to change residences, and he delayed moving into the White House until December. Throughout the fall black crepe shrouded the north front of the White House, while on the interior workers redecorated the state rooms, adding an elevator

and improving the plumbing. Arthur declared December 22 a national day of mourning for President Garfield. The White House reopened on New Year's Day, 1882, to special airs composed by John Philip Sousa, the leader of the Marine Band. Newspaper reporter Emily Briggs, known only as "Olivia" to her readers, offered this account of the scene:

Thoroughly renovated and partially refurbished, the old historic building appears like an antiquated belle rejuvenated by the modern accessories of the toilet. Oriental designs, artistically arranged, give the surroundings a magnificence never attained since a former White House mistress died…. A New Year's reception at the White House forms a picture on the mind never to be forgotten. Precisely at the hour appointed the foreign legations began to assemble and in a brief time the Red Room was filled to overflowing with representatives of the different civilized nations of the globe. The gorgeous costumes worn by these people can only be compared to the plumage of birds which infest the tropical forests.

CHESTER A.
ARTHUR
1881–85
⊗

The urbane Arthur continued to polish the image of the White House and the presidency. The following spring extensive new decorations, designed by Louis Comfort Tiffany, were installed. He also requested Sousa to replace "Hail to the Chief," a piece played for presidential arrivals since John Quincy Adams opened the C&O Canal on July 4, 1828. "Do you find it suitable?" asked Arthur. "No, sir," Sousa replied. "It was chosen years ago largely because of its title." Arthur responded. "Then, change it!" Sousa composed a number entitled "Presidential Polonaise" for indoor affairs and the rousing "Semper Fidelis" for use outdoors. "Presidential Polonaise" was used for a while, but it never fully supplanted "Hail to the Chief" and eventually was dropped from the repertoire.

Arthur continued civil service reforms that had begun with Garfield, including the establishment of Christmas as a federal holiday in 1885.

WHITE HOUSE
SOCIAL OFFICE

In 1881 President Garfield appointed Warren Young head of the first White House social office, which prepared the engrossing on invitations; he held this position until his death in 1917. He was replaced by his understudy, William Rockwell, who managed the office until 1940, when Adrian Tolley, who had been scripting names since 1915, took over the office. Also on the staff was John Lincoln McCabe, who started delivering invitations by bicycle in 1904 and was still working on the invitation list when he retired in 1953.

CHAPTER SEVEN

O Tannenbaum

Grover Cleveland came to Washington as president in 1885, travelling without a wife and with a resolve (like his predecessor, James Polk) to be "the hardest working man in America." Receptions, parties, and even friendly dinners were considered by Cleveland to be tiresome chores. The women of Washington, who took their cues from the White House social season, were required to fend for themselves for the next four years until the Harrison family, who took formal entertaining and domestic proprieties seriously, took their places on Pennsylvania Avenue.

"The guardians of polite society," according to the wife of Joseph B. Foraker, Republican senator from Ohio, "[made their] last stand at the White House. The Harrisons gathered … women who could give all their time to social perfections undistracted by suffrage, divorce, interior decoration or other externalities.… We still exchanged recipes … changed our dresses exhaustingly—often during the day, and were, altogether, as conventional as a sideboard."

Caroline Scott Harrison was the first president of the Daughters of the American Revolution and was considered the soul of

BENJAMIN
AND
CAROLINE SCOTT
HARRISON
1889–93

motherly home economy because of her interest in china painting, needlework, cookbooks, and teatime gossip. Conveniently, the rise of secular and homecrafted Christmas celebrations in Washington occurred at about the time that the Harrisons arrived, providing a perfect rationale for inaugurating yuletide customs at the White House without appearing to violate the concept of separation of church and state. A parallel development to the rise of these homespun Christmas-keeping customs in Washington was the official observance of Christmas as a holiday, a consequence of the the Pendleton Act of 1883, which established the federal Civil Service Commission. The establishment of Christmas Day as a paid holiday for federal workers in 1885 has a curious and obscure history. Although Christmas Day had for some time generally been observed as a holiday, the practice was informal and varied from agency to agency.

Unlike virtually every other country in the world, the United States does not celebrate national holidays. Instead, each state adopts its own observances, along with federal holidays, decreed for employees of the federal government. The legal recognition

Opposite: Red Room, c. 1890. Beginning in the late 1920s, a Christmas tree was set up in the East Room during the holidays as seasonal decoration for parties. Other rooms on the State Floor were generally not decorated until the Eisenhower years, beginning in 1953, when virtually each room in the White House was graced with a tree.

A CITY IN THE WILDERNESS

The United States [is] the only great country in the world which has no capital.... By a capital I mean a city which is not only the seat of political government, but also by its size, wealth and character of its population the head and centre of the country, a leading seat of commerce and industry, a reservoir of financial resources, a favoured residence of the great and powerful, the spot in which chiefs of the learned professions are found, where the most potent and widely-read journals are published, whither men of literary or scientific capacity are drawn.

—James Bryce,
The American Commonwealth, 1888

There were a few amusing and intelligent people living in Washington in the 1890s, including Cecil Spring Rice, a diplomat with the British embassy, Theodore Roosevelt, who (at that time) was a member of the Civil Service Commission, Sen. Henry Cabot Lodge and Henry Adams, who held court at 1603 H Street on Lafayette Square, and the sometime visitor Rudyard Kipling. When Rice went with Roosevelt to visit the Harrisons at the White House, he wrote home that "they were small and fat. They said they were glad to see us, but neither looked it."

of Christmas began in the states and territories with a statute passed in Alabama in 1836, followed by Louisiana and Arkansas in 1838; 25 more states enacted legislation for the observance of Christmas by 1865. The remaining states and territories passed similar statutes at the rate of one a year or so until 1890. The first federal recognition of a Christmas holiday came in 1870, when employees of the District of Columbia were given a paid holiday for December 25. According to James Barnett, "The historical implications of these dates are not conclusive, but indicate that the middle decades of the nineteenth century saw the formal recognition of Christmas Day.... This suggests the disappearance of Puritan opposition to the celebration and its acceptance as a folk festival."

One explanation for the delay in the

creation of a federal holiday (Act of January 5, 1885, as amended 5 U.S.C. 86) relates to Congress's own calendar and pay schedule. For 68 years, from 1789, when it first assembled, until 1856, Congress was officially in session on Christmas Day every year except in 1800, 1817, and 1828. Afterward except during the war years of 1861 and 1862, Congress was in recess during the Christmas holiday each year until 1933, when the calendar was changed for the 73rd Congress; afterward, each session was convened sometime after New Year's Day. It is probably not a coincidence that Congress paid itself on a per diem basis through 1856 (at the rate of eight dollars a day), establishing annual compensation beginning in 1857, the year that congressmen and senators first enjoyed a paid holiday (Act to Regulate Compensation of Members of

Congress, August 16, 1856). Since members of Congress were not paid when they officially took Christmas as a holiday, they may have been reluctant to extend a paid holiday to members of their staffs and those of the executive and judicial branches of government.

Unofficially, of course, the government was closed not only for Christmas Day but also for most of Christmas week. A notice in the *Evening Star* from 1885 reported that at the cabinet meeting yesterday it was decided that the departments should be closed at noon on the days immediately preceding Christmas and New Year and all day on those holidays. During holiday week no other holidays are to be given, and the departments will transact business as usual. This decision was reached because of the backward condition of work at the various departments. It was thought that if any more holidays were granted there would be a serious accumulation of work. This notice suggests a precedent of granting extended paid leave during the Christmas season in previous years.

Col. W. H. Crook, the old White House retainer, noted in his 1901 memoirs that "there had been plenty of young people [at the White House] during previous administrations from Lincoln's down through Johnson's, Grant's, Hayes's, Garfield's, Arthur's, Cleveland's—and plenty of excuse for a Christmas tree," yet the first president actually to put one up in the White House was Benjamin Harrison. The absence of a tree in White House Christmas celebrations during the whole postwar era is best explained by looking at the particular presidential families through the period. All except Arthur were westerners (that is, they hailed from west of the Allegheny Mountains) and evangelicals, belonging to Protestant denominations that were disinclined to lift a glass in Christmas cheer. Lincoln, from Illinois, and Cleveland, from western New York, were Presbyterians; the Johnsons, from Tennessee, and the Hayeses, from Ohio, were members of the Methodist Church, while James Garfield, who was assassinated before his first White House Christmas, belonged to the Disciples of Christ. Family Christmas traditions, such as a decorated tree, travelled from the East Coast westward and spread from Lutherans, Episcopalians, and Catholics to other Protestants, so it is not surprising that the practice of decorating a tree in the White House began with Benjamin Harrison, an Episcopalian and a member of one of the first families of Virginia.

According to Ike Hoover, a White House usher, "wine flowed like water" once again at the President's House. President Harrison was a great friend of Leland Stanford of California, who kept the White House vaults filled with sweet California wine, which was dispensed with lavish

In an *Evening Star* interview published December 24, 1889, an oldtimer remarked that "fifty years ago, when I was a clerk at Treasury, there was no such preparation for Christmas as now. We worked right on, not even having a half day Christmas eve…. We did not even have New Year day, but usually left the building to pay our respects to the President and then forgot to come back. Instead, we would go to each others' houses and drink eggnogg."

Baby McKee (seated in cart) and White House entourage, 1890.

To Prepare Turkey for Christmas Dinner

"The turkey should be cooped up and fed well some time before Christmas. Three days before it is slaughtered it should have an English walnut forced down its throat three times a day, a glass of sherry once a day. The meat will be deliciously tender, and have a fine nutty flavor."

—Mrs. Stephen J. Field, wife of the associate justice of the Supreme Court, from *Statesmen's Dishes and How to Cook Them* (1890), by Mrs. Benjamin Harrison

abandon for four years. Another presidential perquisite was an annual gift from the business tycoon Andrew Carnegie of a 10-gallon keg of John Dewar's best scotch whisky, sent to the White House each year at Christmas beginning in 1891. The practice continued until Woodrow Wilson put a stop to it in 1913.

Benjamin Harrison's presidency drifted quietly into obscurity, sandwiched between Grover Cleveland's two terms. During those years the spotlight of fame shone on his grandson, "Baby" Benjamin Harrison McKee. Baby McKee's mother was Mary ("Mame") Harrison McKee, the president's only daughter, who had moved into the White House with her two children to nurse her mother during an illness from which she never recovered and to serve as White House hostess. At the height of the gilded era, epitomized by the ostentatious display of huge fortunes and glittering, extravagant entertainments, Mame McKee moved deftly into the social whirl with her little Baby McKee at center stage.

Mrs. McKee leaked the plans for the Harrisons' first White House Christmas to the *Evening Star*, which gave it front-page coverage on Christmas Eve, 1889:

Tonight there will be great preparations at the White House. The babies will be put away early and then the President will unbend his official dignity and will lend a hand in the decoration of a glorious Christmas tree that has been erected in the blue chamber, formerly occupied by President Arthur. Along the mantel will hang a row of administration stockings, great and small, filled to a plethoric condition. Tomorrow morning young Benjamin McKee will visit the chamber in pomp, followed by the household, eager for a peak at the wonderful mysteries of Christmas. In fact, it will be just about like other Christmas celebrations in the ordinary houses of the land, lots of joy and good will, abundance of love, a multitude of presents and candy and nuts galore. There will be green boughs and wreaths all over the upper apartments. The President's desk will have a holiday, likewise the President, for an edict has gone forth from the inner domestic sanctum that no work shall be done on the day of days....

Mrs. McKee wrote her own version of the day to her husband on the day after Christmas:

…after breakfast we lighted the tree (almost half past ten) and I do wish you could have seen Benjamin and Mary [her 17-month-old daughter] as I took them into the room. I had the tree put into the room upstairs that we used last year for the nursery. We could darken that so well and as it is not in use at present the children can enjoy the tree for several days. We called all the employees and servants in and I think they were as much pleased as the children. Papa gave each man who has a family a turkey and those who have not, a pair of gloves. We also had some little remembrances for the cooks, laundresses, waiters and those that are immediately around us…. I gave Mama a pair of gold side combs for her hair and Papa a pocket piece—it is a silver dollar so arranged that it opens and contains a place for a picture…. I can hardly enumerate all the children had but by Sunday I will try to send you a list…. I must tell you something of my Christmas—father sent me a twenty-dollar gold piece. His note was the best part of it…. You should see Papa and Benjamin yesterday—they had a mighty happy day together. Your loving wife, Mame.

The cheerful enterprise of home-grown Christmases with the Harrisons continued in succeeding years, with the president dressed as Santa, distributing presents from beneath the candle-lighted tree.

During the Gay Nineties electric lights were installed at the White House and improvements were made in the telephone service, first installed by Alexander Graham Bell during the Hayes years. In addition, the domestic circle widened to welcome Mary Dimmick, 34, Caroline Harrison's widowed niece, who arrived on Christmas Day, 1892, with her son, Scott, and remained to live at the White House. Three years after her aunt Caroline died, she married the 63-year-old Harrison. Their engagement was announced on Christmas Day, 1895, and they were married four months later in New York without the blessing or presence of the groom's children, all whom were older than the bride and outraged by the match.

The first electric Christmas tree lights were installed in 1882 at the New York City mansion of Edward Johnson, an executive of Edison Electric Company.

When Grover Cleveland was first elected president in 1885, he hardly ever stopped working, taking time off only for his wedding, which occurred at the White House in 1886. The 50-year-old Cleveland married his deceased law partner's daughter, 22-year-old Frances Folsom, a young woman of considerable grace and beauty from Buffalo, New York. Between terms their first child, "Baby Ruth," was born, followed during their second White House tour by two more daughters and two sons.

Unlike the Harrisons, the Clevelands were down-to-earth folks who did not care much for society, leading a quiet life at Woodley, in what is now Cleveland Park in residential northwest Washington. It was their home away from the White House, to which they returned only for the social season each year. While their receptions and dinner parties were frequent and impressive, they left the details to staff members, resulting in an impersonal and somewhat stilted presentation.

Although there was no Christmas tree during the first Cleveland administration,

---

GROVER AND FRANCES FOLSOM CLEVELAND 1893–97

⊛

---

the arrival of daughters Ruth, Esther, and Marion prompted the Clevelands in 1895 to set up a tree, replete with electric lights, gold angels with spreading wings, gold and silver sleds, tops of every description, and tinsel. Beneath the tree was a miniature White House, a doll house for Esther, which still remains in her family. (Esther Cleveland Bosanquet, the only daughter of a president to be born in the White House, lived until 1980). Frances Cleveland's principle Christmas activity, rather than entertaining, was her work with the Colored Christmas Club of Washington, D.C., a charity that provided food, clothing, and toys to poor children. She volunteered her time to wrap and distribute gifts to the children, sitting with them for a Punch and Judy show. Although Christmas Club charities in Washington date back to the 1820s and socialite Marcia Van Ness, no previous first lady had taken as active a part in these activities as Frances Cleveland, who helped set a tradition expanded by Lou Hoover and Eleanor Roosevelt and others in their good works.

Opposite: "Santa Claus" Grover by D. McDougall ran in the *New York World,* December 25, 1892.

CHAPTER EIGHT

A Great Big Lovable Teddy Bear

No president of the United States kept Christmas as Theodore Roosevelt did. An irrepressible Knickerbocker with a long family tradition of holiday celebrations in New York, Roosevelt could hardly wait for Christmas to come each year. In Oyster Bay, where he had built Sagamore Hill, a grand Victorian homestead, he presided year after year as Santa Claus at P. S. No. 1, his children's one-room school, dispensing advice and cheer and Christmas presents that he often selected himself.

When Roosevelt was 26 years old, tragedy struck. His mother and his wife died on the same day, February 14, 1884, leaving him with an infant daughter born two days earlier. Two years later he married his childhood playmate, Edith Carow, who gave birth to five children over the next decade while they lived variously in New York City, Oyster Bay, and Washington, D.C.

In 1898 he left his post as assistant secretary of the navy to become a lieutenant colonel in the army, organizing a cavalry regiment known as the "Rough Riders" and leading the charge up San Juan Hill during the Battle of Santiago in Cuba. By November of that year he had been elected gover-

> THEODORE
> AND
> EDITH CAROW
> ROOSEVELT
> 1901–09
> ✿

nor of New York and moved into the governor's mansion on New Year's Eve with Edith and his six children. Edith had caught the flu over Christmas and failed to appear at the governor's reception on New Year's Day. The house was so big that heating it required three men working around the clock to stoke the furnace, which consumed 350 tons of coal that year. Two years later, on Christmas Day, 1900, the Roosevelts moved once more, this time to a house at 1733 N Street in Washington. Roosevelt had been elected vice president, replacing President McKinley's first-term running mate, Adlai Stevenson, Sr. (the latter-day Adlai's grandfather). Roosevelt was controversial. Mark Hannah, chairman of the Republican National Committee and McKinley's sponsor, proclaimed at the convention, "Don't any of you realize there's only one life between this madman and the White House?" Hannah's warnings came true. McKinley was assassinated on September 14, and 42-year-old Roosevelt became president of the United States, moving kit and caboodle—six children, a dog, a cat, a pony, and a pet bird—into the White House on September 27. "Now look,"

Opposite: "General Santa Claus Reviews His Annual Parade," a political cartoon by F. T. Richards appearing in *Collier's Weekly*, December 15, 1906.

CABINET DINNER, DECEMBER 18, 1902

With the Roosevelts, who were accustomed to a large number of household employees, big residences, and plenty of resources, the routine for entertaining large numbers frequently was precise and elegant. Opening their first social season after the restoration of the White House, the Roosevelts gave a dinner for 72 guests, who were seated at a specially built horseshoe-shaped table in the State Dining Room.

The dinner began with Blue Point oysters with brown bread, followed by Kennebac salmon with cucumbers and hollandaise sauce, served with champagne. Sweetbreads à la Matlas, saddle of South Downs mutton with fresh stuffed mushrooms and potatoes dauphine and terrapin à la Baltimore were served, after which a sorbet and roman punch were offered as a refreshing pause before the pièce de résistance, roasted canvasback duck with fried hominy and jelly. Salade Louise then followed with cheese and pull bread, a gracie fantasie, then petits fours glacés, cerises fondantes, peppermints, marrons glacés and bonbons fourrés with a red Bordeaux, ruinart, sherry, Apollinaris water, and liqueurs served by waiters in the appropriate sequence.

Out in the hall the orchestra played numbers such as the Grand Fantasia from Carmen, Lagey's "An Evening Breeze" caprice, Strauss's "Weiner Blut" waltz, Victor Herbert's "Singing Girl," and de Koven's "Foxy Quiller" march.

Dinner ended at 10 o'clock but the men lingered while the Family Dining Room (used as a staging area for the waiters) was readied for port and cigars.

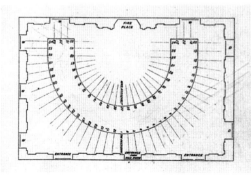

Seating chart for the Roosevelts' cabinet dinner.

An original Ideal Toy Teddy Bear™ is in the collection of the National Museum of American History of the Smithsonian Institution. Soon after its introduction, the teddy bear became one of America's most popular Christmas gifts.

TEDDY ROOSEVELT AND THE TEDDY BEAR

The fable of the teddy bear began in November 1902, when Theodore Roosevelt was on a hunting trip in the South. A *Washington Post* story with a Mississippi dateline carried the headline "One Bear Bagged—But It Did Not Fall a Trophy to President's Winchester"; the next day a Clifford Berryman cartoon depicted Roosevelt refusing to shoot a captured bear. In fact, the animal was a mature black bear weighing 235 pounds that had killed one of the hunting dogs and had already been wounded when the president arrived on the scene. When Roosevelt saw the creature tied to a tree, "he would neither shoot it or permit it to be shot" but suggested to one of his companions to "put it out of its misery." According to the Post account, "[the] President was called [to shoot] after the beast had been lassoed, but refused to make an unsportsmanlike shot." Another hunter in the party did the deed. The cartoon was copied in other newspapers around the country, the bear became a bear cub, and the incident became a cause célèbre.

Morris and Rose Michtom of Brooklyn, New York, saw the cartoon and devised two stuffed bears to put in the window of their stationery and novelty store. The toy bears drew attention from passersby, and Morris decided to produce the bears for sale seeking, and receiving, permission from the president to name these new toys "teddy bears." By 1903 the Michtoms had established a full production line and called their new enterprise the Ideal Novelty and Toy Company. By 1907 dozens of firms were turning out teddy bears, which became the most successful toy in history.

exclaimed Hannah, "that damned cowboy is President of the United States."

In a long letter to James Garfield, son of his secretary of the interior, grandson of former President Garfield, and a playmate of his 11-year-old son, Kermit, Roosevelt described a typical family Christmas:

White House, December 26, 1902.
Jimmikins:
Among all the presents I got I don't think there was one I appreciated more than yours; for I was brought up to admire and respect your grandfather, and I have a very great fondness and esteem for your father. It always seems to me as if you children were being brought up the way that mine are. Yesterday Archie got among his presents a small rifle from me and a pair of riding-boots from his mother. He won't be able to use the rifle until next summer, but he has gone off very happy in the riding boots for a ride on the calico pony Algonquin, the one you rode the other day. Yesterday morning at a quarter of seven all the children were up and dressed and began to hammer at the door of their mother's and my room, in which their six stockings, all bulging out with queer angles and rotundities, were hanging

from the fireplace. So their mother and I got up, shut the window, lit the fire, taking down the stockings, of course, put on our wrappers and prepared to admit the children. But first there was a surprise for me, also for their good mother, for Archie had a little Christmas tree of his own which he had rigged up with the help of one of the carpenters in a big closet; and we all had to look at the tree and each of us got a present off of it. There was also one present each for Jack the dog, Tom Quartz the kitten, and Algonquin the pony, whom Archie would no more think of neglecting than I would neglect his brothers and sisters. Then all the children came into our bed and there they opened their stockings. Afterwards we got dressed and took breakfast, and then all went into the library, where each child had a table set for his bigger presents. Quentin had a perfectly delightful electric railroad, which had been rigged up for him by one of his friends, the White House electrician, who has been very good to all the children. Then Ted and I, with General Wood and Mr. Bob Ferguson, who was a lieutenant in my regiment, went for a three hours' ride; and all of us, including all the children, took lunch at the house with the children's aunt, Mrs. Captain Cowles—Archie and Quentin having their lunch at a little table with their cousin Sheffield. Late in the afternoon I played at single stick with General Wood and Mr. Ferguson. I am going to get your father to come on and try it soon. We have to try to hit as light as possible, but sometimes we hit hard, and today I have a bump over one eye and a swollen wrist. Then all our family and kinsfolk and Senator and Mrs. Lodge's family and kinsfolk had our Christmas dinner at the White House, and afterwards danced in the East Room, closing up with the Virginia Reel.

Like John Quincy Adams before him and William Taft and John Kennedy after him, Roosevelt came from settled circumstances and was, perhaps, born to be president. His mother was a Georgia aristocrat, his father a Dutch burgher. His grandfather, Cornelius Van Schaack Roosevelt, was believed to be the richest man in New York City. From his earliest years Roosevelt seemed to appreciate his place in history and acted accordingly, including preserving

A ROOSEVELT ROMAN HOLIDAY, 1869

During a family trip to Rome in 1869, 11-year-old Roosevelt wrote in his journal:

Christmas! Christmas! hip, hip, hurrah! I was awake at 4 and we all 4 children got up a little before 6 and went in to Mamas and Papas bed. I caught everybody in saying "Merry Christmas." We then opened our stockings. They were nice and bulky. I had 2 oranges and 5 kinds of candy in mine. I had a compas, themometer, 12 photographs, a cardinal's cap. A pair of gloves and a beautiful cravat. Gourd for a water flask. A little ivory box with amber cover and ivory chammois. Then we got dressed and looked over our presents. We then had breakfast... [and] said "Merry Christmas" to Mr. Stevens. Then Papa and Mama came in (we had prayers) and then we had breakfast. We then went in the parlor to our tables. The presents passed our utmost expectations.... I received two lamps and an inkstand on the ancient pompeien style and a silver sabre, slippers, a gold helmet and cannon besides the ivory chammois. I have beautiful writing paper, a candle stick on the Antiuke stile. A mosaic 1,500 years old and 3 books, 2 watch, 9 big photographs and an ornament and pair of stubs....

According to Corinne Robinson, Roosevelt's sister, "Christmas in Rome was made for us as much like our wonderful Christmases at home as possible.... the special joy in the hearts of the three little American children was that they had actually forgotten that they were in Rome at all!"

**CHRISTMAS AT
SAGAMORE HILL, 1895**

Whenever it snowed at Christmas, the Roosevelts would hitch up the sled and drive the short distance to church for services.

his boyhood diary and correspondence. He graduated from Harvard College and studied law at Columbia University before serving in the New York State Assembly and as a deputy sheriff of Billings County in the Dakota Territory. After he ran unsuccessfully for mayor of New York City, Roosevelt was appointed one of the first members of the U.S. Civil Service Commission and then assistant secretary of the navy. After less than a year of military service, he was elected governor of New York in 1899, vice president in 1900, and president of the United States in 1901.

Roosevelt's childhood observations are strikingly similar to those of his adult years. Edith Roosevelt, as first lady, often remarked that she had four wild boys to look after (her husband being the fourth). To a remarkable extent Roosevelt never changed, including his relationship with Edith, who was the best friend of his sister

Corinne as they grew up on Union Square in New York City. Throughout his life, duty and tradition commingled with high jinks and rough-house play to define Teddy Roosevelt.

Roosevelt was delighted with Christmas, "an occasion," he recalled from his childhood,

of delirious joy. In the evening we hung up our stockings—or rather the biggest stockings we could borrow from the grown-ups—and before dawn we trooped in to open them while sitting on father's and mother's bed; and the bigger presents were arranged, those for each child of its own table, in the drawing-room, the doors of which were thrown open after breakfast. I never knew anyone to have what seemed to me such attractive Christmases, and in the next generation I tried to reproduce them exactly for my own children.

In his published letters to his sister Corinne, Roosevelt wrote of one later Christmas, "We had a delightful Christmas yesterday, just such a Christmas as thirty or forty years ago we used to have under Father's and Mother's supervision in 28 East 20th Street." His oldest son put Christmas for the Roosevelts in perspective when he wrote that "in all well-regulated families there are customs so sanctified by time that they cease to be mere customs and rank with the famous laws of Medes and Persians. This holds particularly true when there are large numbers of children."

This emphasis on family Christmas traditions is important in understanding the enormous uproar that was created when the president forbade his two youngest boys, Archie and Quentin, to have a Christmas tree in the White House. At the time nearly every major news daily had articles about this lapse in presidential judgment. The only explanation offered was that the cutting of Christmas trees was injurious to the environment. Supposedly, Roosevelt, as a conservationist, did not want to encourage the wanton distruction of America's forests.

While Roosevelt's public policy rationale for not allowing a tree in his family's Christmas celebration may have rested on environmental concerns, it is clear that he did not want a tree in the White House because his family had not had one in New York when he was a boy. During their years in the White House, the Roosevelts joined Theodore's sister Anna Cowles and her family for Christmas dinner and enjoyed the big tree at their house in suburban Virginia.

The fuss made about the absence of a White House Christmas tree is indicative of how entrenched American Christmas traditions had become by the turn of the century. From the first White House tree for Baby McKee only a decade before, the country had come not only to accept but also to expect Christmas-keeping customs at the White House as part of the national celebration. After a serious conference with Archie and Quentin and his secretary of the interior (who surprised the president by taking the boys' side, explaining that careful,

After first objecting, Roosevelt was persuaded by his environmental advisor, Gifford Pinchot, to admit a tree into the White House. Archie and Quentin set up a small tree with electric lights in their room in 1902, where the family came for an inspection on Christmas morning, the beginning of a family tradition that became one of the rituals of the day.

selective cutting of Christmas trees would not harm the forests), Roosevelt admitted a small tree with electric lights into the boys' room in 1902, and in the following years a family visit to the tree became one of the rituals of the day.

Because of the period of mourning following McKinley's assassination, the Roosevelts did not have a social season during their first year in the White House, although they did begin to entertain almost at once with frequent family-style dinners for 30 or 40 guests. For Roosevelt the prestige of the United States among the nations of the world rested not only on the substance of his policies but also on the style that he and Edith set at the White House. The war with Spain over Cuban independence, a symbol of expansionism, marked a new high point in American influence and opened a new era of U.S. foreign policy. At the dawn of the 20th century several Washington legations became embassies as Europe began to recognize America's new military and economic power.

Col. Theodore Bingham of the U.S. Army Corps of Engineers, who was in charge of Washington's public buildings, was intent on expanding and renovating the White House. After 100 years it was time to provide the president with adequate accommodations for his staff and his family. The eight rooms allotted on the second floor for the official residence were hardly enough for the Roosevelts. Office visitors constantly stumbled into domestic situations, there was little room for storage, and arrangements for servants were inappropriate. In addition, the White House was out of date and in poor repair, requiring constant maintenance inside and out.

A distinguished commission was named to study the building's condition and propose solutions. The commission members included the great architects Daniel H. Burnham of Chicago, designer of the 1893 World's Columbian Exposition in Chicago and later Union Station in Washington, D.C., and Charles F. McKim, a relative of Rutherford B. Hayes and a partner in the prestigious New York firm of McKim, Mead and White; the landscape architect Frederick Law Olmsted, Jr., son of and young apprentice to the designer of Central

Opulent state dinners were almost routine at the Roosevelt White House. This dinner for Prince Henry of Prussia in 1902 featured a 12-course dinner.

Park in New York; and the celebrated sculptor Augustus Saint-Gaudens. After touring the homes and offices of heads of state in Europe, the commission selected one of its own, Charles McKim, to expand and renovate the White House.

The freshly renovated White House officially reopened with a cabinet dinner held on December 18, 1902. The changes were striking. Social callers now entered the building from a new East Wing, walking through an arcade and into the basement level just beneath the State Floor. Business was now conducted in a new "temporary" West Wing structure, where the presidential aides worked, although the president still maintained an office on the second floor of the White House. The vast old greenhouses had been torn down, and interior details—moldings, trim, paneling, fabrics, and fixtures—were completely changed. These changes were cosmetic but reflected serious changes in the nature of the presidency and the White House. The building's official name, the Executive Mansion, was changed to the White House.

Public perceptions of Theodore Roosevelt changed with the proliferation of new technologies after the Spanish-American War. The emergence of motion pictures (1900), the advent of global telegraph (1903) and rural free postal delivery (1904), the expansion of magazine publishing (1904), and the proliferation of photoengraving and radio broadcasting (1906) conspired to present to Americans and to the world the personality of the American presidency. These developments also led to an expansion of advertising and retailing and the resulting merger of regional cus-

toms into national pastimes. Christmas, of course, was a part of the mix.

Inevitably, there was born a White House press corps, which took an interest in both the private and public life of the first family. Although Edith Roosevelt attempted to maintain some measure of privacy, she worked against an American public that increasingly delighted in reading anything and everything about the Roosevelt gang in the White House. While Tad Lincoln, Baby McKee, and Baby Ruth were generally well-known in their time, Alice Roosevelt achieved an unparalleled celebrity from almost the first day of her residency at the White House.

After her first Christmas at the White House, Alice entered society. She recalled in her memoirs:

My coming-out dance was early in January, before the Christmas holidays were over, so carloads of my friends from out of town came down for it. I myself enjoyed it moderately. The crash [of people] in the east room I considered personally humiliating, and

"New Life in the Old House. I Don't Know When I've Felt So at Home Here, " by Thomas Nast, was a gift from the artist the year the Roosevelts moved into the White House. Since the Civil War, Nast had provided an annual Christmas illustration of Santa Claus for *Harper's Weekly* that eventually evolved into the representation we recognize today. Roosevelt had been an admirer of Nast for years. After Nast's own publication went bankrupt, Roosevelt appointed the artist consul to Guayaquil, Equador. When friends asked him why he was going to Guayaquil, he answered that it was to learn how to pronounce its name. Soon after his arrival, Nast, 62, died of yellow fever.

Today a party for the children of diplomats with elaborate entertainments provided by celebrities such as Shari Lewis and Big Bird is a tradition. The first such party, as least on a contemporary scale, was conceived by Edith Roosevelt. In November a letter went out from William Loeb, secretary to the president, to diplomats, members of Congress, and other dignitaries, asking for the names and ages of the minor children, if any, in the family. Mrs. Roosevelt then sent invitations to all the children of official Washington, perhaps 600 in all, ages 6 to 16, indicating simply that she was "at home" on Saturday, December 26, from 4 until 6:30 p.m. Abby Gunn Baker, the Washington journalist closest to Mrs. Roosevelt, filed a story on December 20 in the *Washington Post*, reciting verbatim a memorandum probably prepared by Isabella Hagner, Mrs. Roosevelt's social secretary:

Mrs. Roosevelt has received a number of inquiries as to whether older persons are expected to accompany any of the very young children invited to the party on Saturday, December 26th. In order to answer what appears to be a general desire for information

Admission card to a children's party at the White House, December 26, 1903.

on this point, it may be said that the list of those invited is so large that it is thought it would be better if only in cases where a child is very young and timid an older member of the family should accompany it.... A dressing room downstairs will be provided for any maids who are obliged to wait for their charges.

On the day after Christmas, 550 children arrived at the White House by the East entrance, leaving their wraps in the cloak boxes downstairs and ascending the staircase to the State Floor, where they were introduced to Mrs. Roosevelt by Major McCawley, both of whom were standing at the north door of the Green Room. They were then ushered into the East Room through the southeast door, where they were handed an engraved program and shown a seat. Only 10 or 12 mothers or nannies appeared upstairs with their children.

The East Room was completely filled with chairs, including every available one in the White House and 200 more that had been rented. Entertainment began at 4:20 with Roney's Boy Concert Company, a vaudeville act from Chicago, featuring five young men who, performing on a stage at the north end of the room, sang and danced their way through six costume changes and a number of Christmas carols, patriotic songs, and miscellaneous theatrical numbers. During the show the president slipped into the room and took a seat next to his wife near the Green Room entrance. The

PROGRAM.

1. Quartette, "In this hour of softened splendor" *Pinsuti*
   "Roney's Boys" (in military uniforms).
   Masters Earle Stark, Charlie Lenzen, Glen Wortman,
   Tony Linden.

2. Christmas Carols:
   "God rest you merry, gentlemen," . *Traditional*
   "Good King Wenceslas" . . . *Traditional*
   "As Joseph was a-walking" . . . *George Fox*
   The Boys (in cotta and cassock).

3. Violin, Concerto in E minor—Andante and
   finale . . . . *Mendelssohn*
   Master Edmund Hunnemann.

4. Bolero, "In Old Madrid" . . . . . *Troteré*
   The Boys (in French court costume, period of Louis XV).

5. Organ Chimes, "Christmas Bells Gavotte" *J. Resch*

6. Songs:
   "My old Kentucky Home" . . . *Foster*
   "A Christmas Sleigh Ride" . . . . *Distin*
   (Accompanied by piccolo, wrist bells, and sleigh bells.)
   The Boys (in college gowns).

7. Flute, National Fantasie . . . *Hartmann*
   Master Tony Linden.

8. Quartette, "Tenting Tonight on the Old Camp Ground"
   The Boys (in patriotic costumes).

9. Song, "The Deathless Army" . . . *Troteré*
   Master Charlie Lenzen.

10. Violin, flute, and piano, "Serenade" . *Schubert*
    Edmund, Tony, and Mr. Roney.

11. Songs:
    "A Highland Lad my Love was Born" . *Robert Burns*
    "O'er Blooming Meadows" . . . *Wekerlin*
    (Organ chimes and voices.)
    "Spanish Students' Song" . . . . *Lacome*
    (Accompanied by tambourine. castanets, triangle,
    and violin.)
    "Merry Christmas" . . . . *Henry B. Roney*
    The Boys (in Highland Scottish costumes).
    "My Country 'tis of Thee " (Sung by audience, stand-
    ing, led by the Boys with voices, violins, flute,
    and organ chimes).

CHILDREN'S PARTY.

—

"RONEY'S BOYS" CONCERT COMPANY OF CHICAGO.

HENRY B. RONEY, DIRECTOR.

SATURDAY, DECEMBER 26, 1903.
WHITE HOUSE.

program lasted an hour, after which the door leading to the main corridor and the northeast door of the Green Room were opened. Twenty-five members of the Marine Band in their red jackets played a march from their station in the main vestibule as the children, led by Major McCawley, Colonel Symons, the President and Mrs. Roosevelt, filed into the State Dining Room for supper.

Gunn's article in the *Washington Post* on December 27 describes the decorations:

The dining room was handsomely decorated. On the table at the north end was a beautiful Christmas tree, lighted by scores of party-colored electric lights. The great dining table was decorated with poinsettia blossoms and carnations, and lighted by silver candelabra, capped with Christmas red shades. It was heaped with all such Christmas goodies as appeal particularly to the heart of a child. The ice cream was molded into the form of Santa Claus, and pretty favors were provided for each guest.

Large as the State Dining Room is, it was not quite spacious enough to accommodate 500 chil-dren at one time, with the result that the President's powers of gener-alship were called into play and the overflow party was accommodated in the adjoining red parlor. The President himself dispensed the steamed oysters, which formed the first course of the supper that finished with a small package of bonbons…"

While the guests were dining, the East Room was cleared and the Marine Band moved to the stage, where they played dance music for the children, ending with "Home Sweet Home" at 6:30, the signal that it was time to leave.

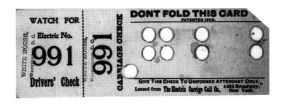

Carriage card for the children's party at the White House.

the fact that punch was provided instead of champagne was a horrid blow to my pride. Moreover, it was just a dance without a cotillion. Other girls had cotillions given for them with … rafts of favors and flowers. That I was a White House débutante hardly made up to me for not having a cotillion!

For Archie, Quentin, and their father every day at the White House was an adventure. Earle Looker, a childhood friend of the boys, told stories of their antics in his book *The White House Gang*:

The first "crime" I remember was directed toward Andrew Jackson, toward his portrait rather, which hung in the upper hall. Some very fine shots were made with spitballs, and very soon Old Hickory was so covered with them that we dragged a chair under the portrait to arrange the wet lumps into designs—three on his forehead, and one on the lobe of either ear.

That night, Roosevelt hauled Quentin out of bed to remove the spitballs, and the next morning, he was at the head of the stairs ready to hold an inquisition. After charges were recited and defenses were laid, Roosevelt found Quentin guilty of launching the first spitball and condemned him to a

week without seeing his friends.

The children were known to roller-skate in the East Room and spy on official guests from the attic through the skylight into the Oval Room. Once they were caught in the act of mimicking the Italian ambassador with his monocle—Quentin, Archie, and their friends were lined up, each with an old watch crystal in his eye, trying to suppress their convulsive giggles.

According to Alice Roosevelt Longworth in her later years, Edwardian society was a "curious, faraway world, much closer to the eighteenth century than life today.… There was a terrible self-consciousness of Americans at the time about the British. They adored and aped everything British." The new wealth and the continuing snobbery of the New York smart set, which included the Roosevelts, and the new status of the White House began to pay off. Beginning with the Roosevelts, 1600 Pennsylvania Avenue finally became the best address and its receptions, musi-

Roosevelt family portrait at the White House, Christmas, 1908. From left: Ethel, Theodore, Jr., Quentin, Mrs. Roosevelt, Kermit, President Roosevelt, Archibald, and Alice and her husband, Rep. Nicholas Longworth. Alice remembered that "we spent our last Christmas at the White House, all the family together, and had our photograph taken on the south portico. If we had any charm at all that photograph certainly does not convey it!"

cales, and dinners the most sought-after social invitations in the country.

Through it all—Alice's and then Ethel's debutante parties, Alice's wedding, the comings and goings of Theodore III, a student at Harvard, and Kermit, a student at Groton—Roosevelt never abandoned his boyish stunts and games. He read endlessly to his children, played blindman's bluff and sticks, and arm-wrestled with them on the floor; he played tennis, went cross-country skiing, and threw snowballs; he jumped on his horse at 3 a.m. one frigid January day and rode with three of his friends to Warrenton, Virginia, and back, a 100-mile trip taking 13 hours. Through the Christmas season one year he made a series of dinner guests, night after night, sit through a movie about wolves that he found fascinating (and Edith found disgusting).

For Teddy Roosevelt the family Christmases with which each year concluded were the epitome of good cheer and good will and seemed to be essential to his being, a time to strengthen the bond with his wife, children, and sisters before setting out to renew his ties with others. The breadth of his experience—adventures throughout the country and the world—became for Americans of his generation a point of pride and measure of success. His gee-whiz enthusiasm and Christmas-keeping ways in the White House went a long way toward popularizing the holiday as a national celebration, further separating its religious aspects from common secular practices.

CHAPTER NINE

Christmas and the American Spirit

The line of presidents from the Midwest that began with Lincoln continued with the Tafts, a family with deep roots in Cincinnati. Nellie Herron, who as a teenager in 1878 declared that she would live in the White House one day, fulfilled her wish 31 years later. For William Taft, his four-year term as president may have been one of the least fulfilling experiences of his life. Handpicked by his friend Theodore Roosevelt, Taft had not run for public office before; his goal was merely to become a justice of the Supreme Court. In fact, it was Nellie, whose father had been Benjamin Harrison's best friend at Miami University (of Ohio) and Rutherford Hayes's law partner, who pushed for the White House.

Early in his term Taft lost the support of Roosevelt while never gaining the hearts of the American voters. In his bid for reelection in 1912, Taft (as well as Roosevelt, who, as a third-party candidate, ran on the Bull Moose ticket) was defeated by former Princeton University president and New Jersey governor Woodrow Wilson. A few years later Warren Harding named Taft to the high court, where he served as chief justice.

However Taft governed the nation, First

> WILLIAM HOWARD
> AND
> HELEN HERRON
> TAFT
> 1909–13
> ✸

Lady Nellie made the best of it, staging glittering affairs that outshone the opulence of even the Roosevelts' soirees, replacing staff and age-old customs with those of a more formal, patrician tone.

Christmas in the Taft White House was probably as close to the Taft family Christmases on Auburn Street in Cincinnati as was practical. Like Roosevelt, Taft was a chip off the old block. As did his father, Alphonso Taft, William went to Yale, became a lawyer, married the daughter of a lawyer, served abroad as a diplomat, was appointed U.S. secretary of war and attorney general, and became a judge.

The Taft family's Christmases included decorated trees as early as 1860 and featured dances, special meals, and lavish rounds of gift giving. On December 14, 1910, the Tafts kicked off the social season with a tea to present their daughter Helen to society. Two thousand invitations were sent, and 1,200 Windsor carnations were brought in for decoration. Two weeks later, amid Nephrolepis ferns and more carnations, Helen had her debutante dance in the East Room; 302 persons attended, including her brother Bob, home from Yale for the holidays.

William Howard Taft.

CHRISTMAS DESSERT

During the Christmas season of 1912, the Baker family of New Jersey presented the first family with an enormous mince pie measuring 3 feet across, 6 feet in circumference, and 2½ inches deep. It was brought into the Family Dining Room by four waiters, who served it to the president and his family at Christmas dinner.

Opposite: A bleak December vista. The likelihood of a white Christmas in Washington is less than one chance in ten, according to the U. S. Weather Service.

In his diary for December 25, 1909, presidential aide Archie Butt wrote this account of a Christmas shopping excursion:

It is a White Christmas in Washington.... My friends have remembered me generously today, but nothing has given me as much pleasure as the book sent me by the President.... We went shopping together yesterday, and it was a regular lark....

The streets were crowded. Very few people noticed the President, and those who did merely raised their hats and said "Merry Christmas" in passing. At the Willard we ran head on into four convivial spirits emerging from the cellar bar of that hotel. "Merry, Merry Christmas" to them, they righted, and with a "Merry Christmas, Missure President, " passed on for the next saloon, laughing uproariously....

We went in at Galt's and the President called for some travelling bags. There was only one and the price was a hundred dollars. I insisted that it was too heavy and too costly, and suggested, much to the chagrin of the salesman, going to Becker's on F Street, where they kept a larger supply. We went out Eleventh Street and then up F. It was the first time he had been on F Street since his inauguration and he enjoyed every minute of it. He said he felt like running.

At Becker's we found the bags to be costly, but finally the President saw one for seventy-five dollars which he liked very much. He said he wanted two and would get this one and the other one at Galt's. I still persisted that it was too much to pay and finally he said:

"You go to the devil, Archie. This or the other one is for you; now do you like it or not?"

I was really abashed, for it never entered into my head that he was going to give me a present, so I said:

"Mr. President, I don't want you to give me anything but what you have already given me, your confidence and your good will."

"Do you like this bag or not, that is what I want to know?" he said.

"Of course I like it, sir."

"Do you like it better than anything else you see?"

"Yes, sir," I answered again.

"Do you like it better than anything else you don't see?"

I hesitated and finally said: "Mr. President, you are not to be dissuaded from giving me something?"

"Do you like it better than anything else you see?"

I hesitated and finally said: "Mr. President, you are not to be dissuaded from giving me something?"

"I am not," he said. "Now out with it."

"Well, if you are determined to give me something, I would rather have some memoirs down at Brentano's than anything else."

"Good," he said, laughing. "Down to Brentano's we go." And we left the store, the salesman looking broken-hearted.

Brentano's was crowded, but we edged our way in and I found at last Mr. Norman, the manager, waiting on someone else. I whispered to him to come and wait on the President. He asked what he could do with the other customer.

"Drop him and let him stand," I said, and we left the customer, a well-dressed, nice-looking man, evidently a gentleman, perfectly bewildered. We made our way to the shelves where the memoirs were to be found, and as we passed through the crowd one man spoke to the President and reached out his hand. I simply gave him a punch in the stomach and hissed "Fool" to him under my breath. The President asked me after we left what I had done to him.

"Oh, I only whispered to him not to begin to shake hands, that it would start the whole store doing it."

...[After purchasing the book] we went back to Galt's, where the President bought a silver-mounted pin-cushion for Mr. Winthrop and some silver knives for the secret service men. By this time it seemed that everybody was cognizant that the President was out shopping, for he was recognized on all sides. No one attempted to interfere with his personal liberty, and yet everyone who saw him wished him a Merry Christmas. It was really quite exhilarating and joyous. He had his fun, too. Whenever he would make a purchase he would say, "Please charge that to me," and would ask: "Do you know who I am? " or "Is my credit good? " and when he wanted something sent to the White House he would say, "Send that to me," and add: "Do you know my address?" or "Do you know where I live?"

Hecht Company dry goods store, founded in 1869 by Baltimore merchant Alexander Hecht, opened before Christmas in Washington, offering silk mufflers and camel's hair shawls, kid gloves and linen handkerchiefs. The following year in New York, Frederick August Otto Schwarz, 34, opened a toy shop on Broadway at 9th Street.

Each party, dinner, reception, golf outing, horseback ride, and shopping trip conducted by Taft seems to have been arranged, witnessed, and remembered by the indomitable Capt. Archibald Butt, social aide extraordinaire, who came to the White House during Roosevelt's elected term. During the next several years he recorded with detailed commentary every moment of every day spent in the president's presence. Just before Christmas for two years in a row the president and Captain Butt walked down F Street for some shopping, stopping at the Hecht Company, Galt's, Garfinckel's, Brentano's, and Bon Marché. On one Christmas shopping excursion to Galt's jewelry store, Butt wrote that he had visited the store earlier in the day to preselect a number of gifts for the president to choose from. He later returned with Taft, who spent half the afternoon buying a gold cigarette case, a cigar cutter, and a few other items, covering only a third of his list. On another occasion Taft bought at Brentano's a copy of *Mad Rulers and Raging Mysteries of a Submissive People* for his friend Gen. Clarence Edwards, inscribing it, "To Clarence, with love, from one of them." During the Wilson administration Butt, exhausted from his work, went on a vacation and never returned, a victim of the sinking of the *Titanic*.

Woodrow Wilson and his first wife, Ellen Louise Axson, were married in her hometown of Savannah, Georgia, by her grandfather and father and his father, all of whom were Presbyterian ministers. They had three daughters—Margaret, who sang to the troops in World War I; Jessie, who married Francis Sayre at the White House in 1913 and was the mother of Francis Bowes Sayre, later distinguished rector of the National Cathedral; and Eleanor ("Nell"), who married her father's secretary of the treasury, William Gibbs McAdoo, also in a White House wedding in 1914. That same year Ellen died of Bright's disease.

The Wilson White House before World War I managed to establish an easy informality in its entertainments. Belle Hagner, who as a child travelled with Ulysses and Julia Grant on the Pacific leg of their post-presidential trip around the world, was installed as the first permanent social aide to a first lady. She was later assisted by Wilson's cousin, Helen Bones, who lived at the White House and who became fast friends with Edith Bolling Galt, a well-to-do Washington businesswoman and the widow of Norman Galt, whose family owned the venerable downtown jewelry store. Edith was the first woman in Washington to own an automobile, a little electric run-about, and she and Helen could be found out and about almost every day. Only a few months after Ellen Wilson's death, Helen introduced Edith to the president, who began courting her the day they met.

There had been no Christmas celebrations at the Reverend Wilson's Presbyterian manse in Staunton, where Woodrow was born, nor in Augusta, Georgia, Columbia, South Carolina, or Wilmington, North Carolina, where the family later moved.

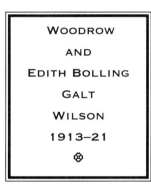

WOODROW
AND
EDITH BOLLING
GALT
WILSON
1913–21
❁

Ten quarts of double cream whipped very stiff, twelve dozen eggs, six quarts of Bourbon whiskey, one pint of rum. For one dozen eggs, use one quart double thick cream, nearly one quart whiskey and two tablespoons of Jamaican rum. Beat the yolks to a cream, add a dessert spoon of sugar with each egg and whip again. Then add whiskey and rum slowly. The cream should be whipped very stiff, and so should the whites of the eggs. Even mixed it will remain indefinitely without separating. It is too thick to be drunk. Serve from a punch bowl into cups with spoons.

Woodrow Wilson and Edith Bolling were married on December 18, 1915.

Mr. Woodrow Wilson

and

Mrs. Norman Galt

née Edith Bolling

announce their marriage

on Saturday the eighteenth of December

nineteen hundred and fifteen

Washington, D.C.

Virginia Roots

Edith Bolling Galt, like Wilson, was a Virginian, he from Staunton, she from Wytheville. Wilson's father was a Princeton graduate before him, and two of his six uncles were Confederate generals during the Civil War. Edith was a direct descendant of Pocahontas and John Rolfe. Five generations later, the Rolfes' descendant, John Bolling, married Thomas Jefferson's sister Martha, with whom he had 11 children, including Edward, Archibald, and Robert, three brothers who married three Payne sisters. Archibald and Jane Payne Bolling were the parents of William H. Bolling, Edith's father.

When Wilson married Edith Galt at her home at 1308 20th Street, at 8:30 p.m. on December 18, 1915, the embellishments of the day were decidedly un-Christmaslike. Edith wore a black velvet dress with a silver belt and fine net sleeves and carried a bouquet of orchids and lilies of the valley. Her diamond brooch was a gift from the president. A profusion of pink flowers—roses, orchids, and lilies—were framed by a canopy of Scottish heather, asparagus vines, Farlayense, and maidenhair ferns. The Marine Band played the Mendelssohn wedding march as the president and his bride descended the stairs.

To escape the crowds that gathered at Union Station to see them off, the couple zig-zagged in their Pierce Arrow through dark back streets to Alexandria, Virginia, parking in the dark shadows next to the rails until their train arrived. They then stepped into a private car that took them to the Homestead in Hot Springs, Virginia,

arriving at seven o'clock the next morning.

Christmas has always been a festive time at the Homestead. In those days the tower had not yet been built, and the Wilsons were ensconsed in four charming rooms filled with flowers on the third floor of the west wing of the hotel, where they could look out their screened porch onto the golf course. Snow had fallen the night before, and the mountains were gleaming white in the morning sun. After breakfasting in their rooms, the newlyweds wrote a few notes to their families. Edith wrote to her mother, "The weather is cold but radiant, and so are we."

The weather turned balmy, and the first couple played golf every morning and took hikes and motored through the mountains in the afternoons. On December 28 they celebrated the president's birthday. Their entourage included their Secret Service agent Edward Starling, who doubled as a driver, a secretary who sent and received messages from the hotel's telegraph office, and a maid and a messenger. On New Year's Day they greeted the other guests and visitors from the surrounding community in the main reception hall. Joining them in receiving were the W. H. Vanderbilts, the Averell Harrimans, and the J. H. McColloughs of New York and Newport.

The Wilsons' wedding trip marked the first time that the president of the United States was not in residence at the White House during the Christmas season since the Madisons had been burned out by the British a century earlier. Because of pressing business relating to the war in Europe, the Wilsons returned to Washington on January 4, several days earlier than planned.

By the next Christmas, 1917, the president had been reelected, but his plan to "establish a league of nations to ensure peace and justice throughout the world" had been rejected not only by other world powers but also by the U.S. Senate. Allied and German soldiers retrieved their dead comrades from frozen trenches at Verdun. At the White House security was tightened, and public access was limited. After Christmas Wilson issued his Ten Points to Congress, and by midyear Americans were leaving on troop ships for Europe. By the next holiday season the country and the White House were observing "wheatless" Mondays and "meatless" Tuesdays. The president's Pierce Arrow was put up on blocks to save fuel, and he began travelling in an ancient horse-drawn victoria found in the White House stables, accompanied by a security detail of uniformed policemen on bicycles. Just before Christmas, 1918, the *Washington Post* declared that "Washington society had given itself up to the war and to charity work." The grand dining table for the State Dining Room was removed and replaced with a small round table from the kitchen to provide a more intimate setting for guests.

On December 4, 1918, a month after the Armistice was signed, Edith and Woodrow Wilson left Hoboken pier on the *George Washington* to spend their Christmas with the troops in France. Edith remembered the falling snow and the line of army cars, led by General Pershing, waiting to take them to the countryside: "The boys made a pitiful attempt to decorate for Christmas with a few green sprays, and little bits of red paper ... they were all so brave, and things were so lonely and uncomfortable, that they brought tears to our eyes despite their efforts to pretend they were full of Christmas cheer." The presidential entourage proceeded to Humes, where a small grandstand had been erected on an open field. Edith described the scene: "What a picture unrolled before us: the brisk marching and counter-marching of the troops through the mire, led by spirited music from the band ... then the cavalry ... then the artillery ... drawn by stout army mules which at times stuck their feet firmly in the mud and refused to move ... and last came the highly camouflaged tanks crawling and bumping over hillocks." The review of the troops was followed by a big Christmas dinner, with turkey, cranberry sauce, and "pumpkin pie cut army fashion in slices as large as this page...." The next day at Charing Cross station King George and Queen Mary were at the step of the train to meet the Wilsons, who were whisked away in two gilded coaches, each drawn by four white horses, to Buckingham Palace, where they were entertained for three days before returning to Paris, then to Rome and other points. Arriving back in Washington after their 10-week trip, the Wilsons returned to a city and country that in their absence had ratified a constitutional amendment outlawing alcoholic beverages. Later that year Wilson rejected the Volstead Prohibition Enforcement Bill, but Congress voted to overide his veto. In October President Wilson suffered a stroke but remained in office for another 20 months. He and Edith retired in 1921 to 2340 S Street, N.W., in the nation's capital and now a property of the National Trust for Historic Preservation.

Until the war the White House maintained a labor-intensive assortment of services, including a full-time staff person who tended the fireplaces in the winter, another who only polished floors, and two clockwinders to keep the 35 to 40 White House clocks wound and set to the correct time.

On the afternoon of Christmas Eve, 1916, 30,000 people, including President and Mrs. Wilson, gathered to hear children from local public schools and Girl Scout troops lead them in carols and patriotic songs, accompanied by the Marine Band on the south steps of the Treasury Department. Margaret Wilson, daughter of the president, was the featured soloist for one of the carols.

During the 1920 presidential campaign one of the candidates running against Harding was labor leader Eugene V. Debs, who ran on the Socialist ticket while incarcerated in the federal penitentiary in Atlanta and garnered 920,000 votes. Debs had objected to America's participation in the war effort and had been sent to prison for publicly denouncing the government's prosecution of people charged with sedition under the Espionage Act of 1917. Wilson had refused to pardon Debs, insisting that the man was a traitor. Harding, however, pardoned Debs and two dozen other political prisoners on Christmas Day, 1921, inviting Debs to stop by the White House on his way home to Indiana. Debs arrived the next day and talked to Harding about prison conditions. As he was leaving the White House, reporters asked him how he liked the president and the White House. He responded, "Mr. Harding appears to be a kind gentleman. One who, I believe, possesses human qualities. We understood each other perfectly. As for the White House [he broke into a grin] well, gentlemen, my personal preference is to live privately as a humble citizen in my cottage in Terre Haute."

At the Republican convention in 1920 Harding was selected over Calvin Coolidge, governor of Massachusetts, and went on to trounce James Cox in November, just before a bedridden Wilson was awarded the Nobel Prize for Peace. Unlike his three predecessors—Roosevelt, Taft, and Wilson—who were born in the 1850s, Harding was born after the Civil War, a member of the generation that was often more attuned to personal profit than public progress.

As the owner of the Marion, Ohio, *Star*, and as U. S. senator from Ohio, Harding was friendly with Ned and Evalyn Walsh McLean. Ned was an heir of the family that owned the *Cincinnati Enquirer* and the *Washington Post*. They had been introduced around a poker table at Alice Roosevelt Longworth's house, and Harding later became a regular member of a foursome that played golf at Friendship, the McLean estate in the Washington suburbs.

Evalyn remembered Christmas, 1922, with the Hardings, who did not have any children and lived alone at the White House:

Once, just before a snowy Christmas, a stream of threatening letters poured into the White House. A sort of final warning was delivered in which some mysterious enemy boasted that on Christmas Day the thing would happen. Mrs. Harding said to me, "Evalyn, we want to spend that day somewhere else...."

"You come and stay with us," I said. (We were living in the I Street house [an enormous mansion designed by John Russell Pope for Ned's parents]).

They went to church and then drove to our

house. We had lunch, then sat around and talked until dinnertime. After dinner we put the President upstairs in a sitting room connected with my bedroom. Up there, we all decided, would be the safest place.

Weeks, Harry Daugherty, Ned, and Charlie Curtis kept him company at bridge or poker. Downstairs, Mrs. Harding and I had a private picture show—Mary Pickford in "Little Lord Fauntleroy." I know that Harding's mind was quite at ease. I heard him laugh a time or two, and threaten what would happen to his friends when he held better cards; but Mrs. Harding twitched and jumped about. She was convinced that at any instant something of first-page moment would happen to them. Outside our house secret-service men were watching, inside the house were others. I always felt a good deal safer when those men were around.

Suddenly, somewhere in the house there was a loud crashing. Mrs. Harding half-screamed and almost slid from her chair. There was no comedy about her fears; they were too real. A servant came in response to my loud calls and apologized because a door had slammed.

About two in the morning the Hardings left, and drove home to the White House. Mr. Harding, shaking hands with me, amusement in his eyes, said, "I'm very grateful to my assassins for a very pleasant Christmas Day." Of course, he had not worried for a minute.

In the middle of his term Harding died of a sudden heart attack during a trip to San Francisco, and the presidential mantle passed to the frugal Yankee John Calvin Coolidge, as taciturn as Harding was expansive. Coolidge, a descendant of John

Coolidge, a Watertown selectman who arrived in Massachusetts in 1630, had worked his way through the political system. Born in Vermont, he became a member of the Massachusetts bar, practicing in Northampton, and began his political career with election to the common council and then city solicitor. He then served as a member of the state house of representatives, mayor, state senator, lieutenant governor and governor of Massachusetts, and eventually as Harding's vice president.

Coming home from military school for their first White House Christmas in 1923, the popular Coolidge boys, Butch and Cal, were given an old-fashioned Christmas by their mother, who lived out her White House holiday fairy tale with all the fancy trimmings. Earlier that month Coolidge had become the first president to address the nation over radio, delivering his message to a joint session of Congress on December 6 through a hook-up to stations in Washington, D.C., New York City, St. Louis, Kansas City, Dallas, and Providence. The first lady entered the House chamber accompanied by Mrs. Charles Evans Hughes, wife of the secretary of state, and Ailsa Mellon, daughter of the secretary of the treasury, to the cheers of the assembly. Edith Roosevelt and Edith Wilson were present, along with Alice Roosevelt Longworth and Lou Henry Hoover, wife of the secretary of commerce. According to her biographer, Isabel Ross, Grace Coolidge had a fabulous Christmas that year:

The President took young Calvin window-shopping. Mrs. Coolidge explored stores for gifts for her family and friends. A spruce tree was set up in the Blue Room and there she gave a dance for sixty boys, doing a turn with each of them. She distributed gifts at Salvation Army headquarters; visited the Walter Reed Hospital to cheer the veterans; sent sixty poinsettias to her church; and she and the President shared in Christmas greetings to all the children of the United States.

In the meantime the simmering Teapot Dome scandal reached the boiling point as the president steadfastly opposed the dismissal of Attorney General Harry Daugherty, Harding's friend from Marion days, who was implicated in the corruption.

While the first lady was busy with holiday preparations and the president with

JOHN CALVIN
AND
GRACE GOODHUE
COOLIDGE
1923–29
⚜

Just before Christmas, 1924, New York City's R. H. Macy Company opened a 20-story department store two blocks west of its Herald Square flagship store. The Macy's Thanksgiving Day parade was created at its new store to launch the Christmas season. Space added in 1928 and 1931 made Macy's the largest department store in the world.

The popular Grace Coolidge was involved in a variety of activities as first lady, after service as national president of the Girl Scouts of America.

affairs of state, C. Bascom Slemp, secretary to the president, received the following letter on November 30, 1923, from Lucretia Walker Hardy, acting general director of the community center department of the public schools for the District of Columbia: "In an entirely informal way, I would like to ask what you think of a plan to have a Christmas tree in the White House grounds under the auspices of the Community Center Department of the Public Schools of the D.C.?" Hardy went on to say that "the residence of the President is affected with the same democracy which permeates all of our institutions.... The tree would be an outward evidence of the President's desire to give encouragement to the spirit of which [Christmas] is symbolical." She proposed setting up a large, electrically lighted tree on the White House grounds near the south fence, providing space for crowds on the Ellipse. Choral singing on Christmas Eve would be arranged, with only the chorus admitted to the White House grounds.

Slemp invited Hardy to the White House for a meeting on December 4 and offered the Ellipse rather than the White House grounds for the community Christmas tree. Mrs. Coolidge had already arranged for 65 choristers accompanied by the Marine Band to carol on December 24 on the North Porch of the White House, and the public would be invited onto the grounds.

Hardy pressed her case in another letter, dated the day of the meeting: "As you will see from the attached blue-print, we want the tree only six feet within the iron fence on the Ellipse side of the White House." Her plea included an opinion from an engi-

neer from Potomac Electric Power Company that "certain physical disadvantages will be avoided if the tree can be placed within the White House enclosure." She also mentioned the fact that the 60-foot cut fir would be furnished by Middlebury College in Vermont and ended her letter with "the cherished hope of associating the tree with the residence of the Nation's Executive." Slemp stood his ground in a response written the same day, stating that it did not seem practical to have more than one event on the White House grounds on the same day.

A compromise was reached: The tree would be placed on the Ellipse, but the president would light it from a remote electric button inside the White House, thereby tying the event directly to the office of the president. A four-piece Marine Band (consisting of two cornets, one euphonium, and one trombone), after completing an assignment on the north side of the White House, would remove the music stands and instruments to the Ellipse for a reprise of its holiday repertoire. As arrangements were being made, Sen. Frank Greene of Vermont requested to be appraised of the developments. On December 20 Hardy wrote another letter, this one to the president. She reported that the button and wiring would cost 500 dollars, a prohibitive amount, and requested that the president appear in person to light the tree. Slemp replied that if the schedule permitted, the president would indeed walk down to the Ellipse at 5:00 to light the tree, which he did at 5:05.

From this rather tentative beginning, the lighting of the national Christmas tree has become one of the most enduring

Christmas traditions at the White House. The following year, 1924, the Christmas tree was a living spruce, planted in Sherman Park immediately south of the Treasury Building, where it remained for nine years. In 1934 another living tree was planted in Lafayette Park, where it served until Christmas, 1939, when the event was moved back to the Ellipse for two years and cut trees were used. In 1941, the first year that the tree was called the national Christmas tree (previously it was called the District of Columbia community or municipal tree), the Secret Service moved the ceremony to the South Lawn, where two alternating living trees continued to be used for the lighting ceremony until 1953. From 1954, the first year that the ceremony was called the Pageant of Peace, until 1972 a cut spruce or fir tree was sent each year from a different state. Since then, a live spruce has served as the National Community Christmas Tree.

By 1925 the Christmas Eve celebration at the National Community Christmas Tree was broadcast over the radio. The program began at 5:50 p.m. with the Marine Band playing Tobani's "Around the Christmas Tree" and included choral renditions of "O Little Town of Bethlehem" and "O Come, All Ye Faithful," the lighting of the tree by the president, and the singing of "Holy Night," piped in over telephone lines through a loud speaker from the community Christmas tree celebration at Madison Square in New York. The ceremonies ended at 6:25 with the singing of the "Star Spangled Banner."

On New Year's Day, 1926, President Coolidge wrote to his father: "I suppose I am the most powerful man in the world, but great power does not mean much except great limitations. I cannot have any freedom even to come and go. I am only in the clutch of forces that are greater than I am. Thousands are waiting to shake my hand today." Coolidge greeted 3,100 visitors that afternoon and later an additional 150 members of the public who arrived too late for

On December 24, 1930, Peggy Ann Hoover and Herbert Hoover III, Hoover's two grandchildren, received a Christmas card delivered to the White House by Kitty Murray and Harry Holme, Jr., bearing the greetings of thousands of children of the capital.

the reception. The president ordered another trumpet fanfare and marched back into
the Blue Room with Grace, dressed elegantly in gray chiffon.

The stock market crashed
during the Hoovers' first
year in the White House, and
a series of economic disasters
followed. The Great Depres-
sion wiped out much of the
affluence of Hoover's constituency, leaving a great deal
of disillusionment in its wake.
A model of the rugged individual, Hoover had built success from the
ground up. An accomplished engineer and
businessman, he had amassed a fortune
before entering public service during World
War I. After the Armistice he became head
of the European relief effort under Wilson.
After the Paris Peace Conference, Franklin
D. Roosevelt, then assistant secretary of the
navy, remarked: "He is certainly a wonder,
and I wish we could make him President of
the United States." Unlike most of his pre-

decessors, Hoover had no experience in
elected office before the presidency, and it
was only happenstance that he became a
Republican.

Hoover and Lou met at Stanford University, where they were both honor students, and married in 1899 on the eve of
their departure to China, where both
worked as geologists near Tientsin. In time
Lou Henry learned to speak five languages
fluently, and together they travelled the
world, settling in London before the war. In
1922 Harding named Hoover secretary of
commerce, and the couple moved to Washington, settling at 2300 S Street, not far
from Woodrow and Edith Wilson and Alice
Roosevelt Longworth. For many years Lou
played Mrs. Santa Claus for the patients at
Children's Hospital and became one of the
leading Washington hostesses during the
Roaring Twenties.

As a cabinet wife and later
as first lady, Lou Hoover began
a tradition of leadership activities outside the White House
that inspired her successor,
Eleanor Roosevelt. Mrs.
Hoover became president of
the Girl Scouts of America and
was active with the National Amateur Ath-
letic Foundation. During their tenure at the
White House the Hoovers dispensed with
many of the formalities that were remnants
of the Victorian era. In his memoirs Hoover
complained that

Harding and Coolidge seemed to be bent on restor-
ing the old customs [abandoned by the Wilsons]—
of receiving a host of public callers.... One of these
ordeals was a noon reception at the White House
office six days in the week, where any citizen might

**HERBERT C.
AND
LOU HENRY
HOOVER
1929–33**

shake the hand of the president if he passed the Secret Service inspection for respectability and harmlessness.... The average of 30 to 40 persons per day at Theodore Roosevelt's receptions had increased to between 300 and 400 per day under Coolidge. And I soon found myself wasting a whole hour every day shaking hands with 1,000 to 1,200 people.

The New Year's Day reception had also gotten out of hand. On the morning of January 1, 1930, the Hoovers woke up to discover that a long line of people had been waiting outside in the bitter cold since midnight. Hoover recounted:

Not to keep the people waiting, Mrs. Hoover suggested that we begin at once. Before the day was over I had shaken hands with over 9,000 people—three times the usual number.... I concluded that the custom might have properly originated with [John] Adams [who received 135 visitors on January 1, 1801], but that he did not know that the population would increase from 3,000,000 to 130,000,000 nor what changes there would be in transportation for visitors into Washington.

Perhaps the most memorable Christmas moment during the Hoovers' tenure in the White House came on December 24, 1929, as they sat around the table in the State Dining Room, entertaining guests at a dinner party. As a liveried waiter was serving the dessert wine to the guests, a siren went off, and an aide rushed in to announce that the White House executive offices in the West Wing were on fire. As the 12-piece Marine Band played on, the guests donned their coats and went out into the snow to watch the District of Columbia fire department arrive and put out the flames. The fire was brought under control in a few minutes, and the guests returned to their sauterne, coffee, and the Hoovers' cheerful repartee.

George Edward Akerson, assistant secretary of commerce, was present at the White House for dinner with his three children on the night of the fire. The following year Mrs. Hoover presented the children with a Christmas present—a model fire truck—as a remembrance of an evening that they were not likely to forget.

The White House fire, December 24, 1929, did considerable damage to the West Wing executive offices but did not reach the residence or the state rooms.

CHAPTER TEN

Eleanor's Year-Round Christmases

As Franklin and Eleanor Roosevelt moved from the governor's mansion in Albany, New York, to the White House, the people of the United States were undergoing a profound examination of their values and their priorities. The nation's economy was in a shambles and unemployment had reached 25 percent.

With perhaps the exception of her Uncle Theodore, no one entered the White House with greater understanding of its opportunities and responsibilities than Eleanor Roosevelt. Eleanor's father, Elliott Roosevelt, was Theodore's younger brother. Both her parents had died in their early thirties, leaving Eleanor an orphan at age 10, to be raised by her grandmother and groomed by her uncles and aunts. "Eleanor was my brother Ted's favorite," remembered Corinne Robinson.

Beginning when she was 16, "Miss Eleanor," as she was called by Ike Hoover, an electrician who became the first chief usher at the White House and stayed on for 42 years, was a frequent visitor to the White House when her uncle and aunt were in residence. At age 21, in 1905, she was married in New York City, with Uncle Teddy at her

> ## FRANKLIN D. AND ELEANOR ROOSEVELT 1933–45
> ❁

side to give her away to Franklin, his godson and Eleanor's fifth cousin once removed, a handsome young Harvard graduate studying law at Columbia University and one of the Hyde Park Roosevelts, the less distinguished branch of the family. Franklin had been determined to fill his godfather's shoes, following him to Harvard (TR graduated in 1880, FDR in 1903) and Columbia University Law School. He then served as a member of the New York State Legislature in Albany (TR served in the lower chamber from 1882 to 1885, FDR in the senate in 1910); as assistant secretary of the navy (TR under McKinley, FDR under Wilson); and as governor of New York (TR served from 1899 to 1900, FDR from 1929 to 1933). Both were candidates for vice president (TR in 1900, FDR in 1920) and served as president (TR from 1901 to 1909, FDR from 1933 to 1945). While Franklin and Eleanor were only barely kissing cousins, Franklin and former President Grant were actually closer relatives (fourth cousins once removed), through Jonathan Delano (1647–1720) and Mercy Warren (granddaughter of Richard Warren, who sailed on the *Mayflower*). Delano was

Opposite: The Roosevelts' Christmas card, 1932, sent from the governor's mansion in Albany, New York.

The president enjoys Christmas, 1937, at the White House with two of his grandchildren.

Grant's grandfather's great-grandfather and FDR's great-grandfather's great-grandfather.

Perhaps of greater significance was the sense of tradition and public service shared by the Roosevelt women. While Eleanor Roosevelt was famous for philanthropies and her Christmas spirit as first lady, she was raised in a tradition of public service long before she met Franklin. Eleanor's aunts—Corinne (Conie) Roosevelt Robinson, Anna (Bye) Roosevelt Cowles, and Edith—were highly intelligent and successful women, seriously engaged in a broad range of public activities. Robinson was a member of the executive council of the Republican National Committee, founded the first wartime Red Cross chapter in 1914, and served on advisory committees for the Coolidge and Hoover administrations. Her husband was a descendant of president James Monroe, and she was the grandmother of newspaper columnists Joseph and Stewart Alsop. Edith also was an active Republican; she was outraged when Franklin ran for president as a Democrat and campaigned for her friend Herbert Hoover in 1932. Although Eleanor became the prototype for progressive career women associated with the Democratic Party, her

public role as first lady certainly derived more from Republican Lou Henry Hoover (who had been her friend and neighbor and whose husband served with Franklin in the Wilson administration) than from Democrats Edith Wilson or Frances Cleveland.

Perhaps because of her bleak childhood at her grandmother's and Allenwood, her English boarding school, Eleanor loved Christmas, finding time to shop for holiday gifts throughout the year. Beginning in 1922 and continuing until her death 40 years later, Eleanor maintained a detailed chronicle of her Christmas gifts, listing more than 200 names with entries in two loose-leaf volumes. She listed the following gifts to her daughter Anna over a six-year period:

1935 books, wrapper, ½ box oranges and grapefruit

1936 6 hankies, lounging pajamas, stocking things (s.t.), walnut mirror

1937 $100 check, material (hand-woven), s.t.

1938 sofa; fur jacket

1939 pearls, s.t. 6 hankies

1940 old silver sugar bowl; stockings; sheets; s.t.

Mrs. Roosevelt's gift entries are charming and banal, extravagant and homey. She loved American crafts (she owned a furniture cooperative at her retreat, Val-kill, near Hyde Park) and simple, practical things. For White House journalist Bess Furman she listed a salad bowl for 1937, a slip and panties for 1938, homespun fabric for 1939, and fruit for 1940. For her friend Lorena Hickok in 1936 she listed "6 handkerchiefs, a desk, and a chintz cover for chair." By 1940, when they had became closer, she listed "a fur coat, oranges and raisins." For scores of acquaintances she rotated maple syrup with mail-order fruit from Harry and David's Orchard, cheese, honey, and nuts. Close female friends received handkerchiefs and, during the war, silk stockings; family members received furniture, toys, books, ash trays, and money (usually 25, 50, or 100 dollars).

The president's Christmas list was much shorter and his gift selection more prosaic. In 1940 he ordered 212 Scottie key chains from Hammacher-Schlemmer in New York. For his last Christmas he ordered his "D-Day Prayer" specially printed and matted for his wife, Secretary of State Cordell Hull, Prime Minister Winston Churchill, Vice President John Garner, Postmaster Jim Farley, Assistant Secretary of State Archibald MacLeish, presidential advisor Bernard Baruch, Gen. George C. Marshall, and others.

During the war Roosevelt became personally interested in his grove of Christmas trees on his estate in Hyde Park and on leased acreage nearby (on his Dutchess County, New York, voting card Roosevelt listed his profession as "farmer"). William Plog, the estate manager, enlisted Nelson Brown of the New York State College of Forestry to help market and manage the grove. The scale of the operation was impressive. "I have ordered 30,000 trees divided equally among Norway spruce, balsam fir, Canadian white spruce and Douglas fir for next spring's planting," Brown wrote to Roosevelt in October 1943.

During that year an offer to sell several hundred trees went out to A&P, Safeway, Macy's, Bloomingdale's, and other stores. The following year A&P harvested the crop at from $.70 to $1.10 per tree, depending on its height. Roosevelt also gave trees to friends. In a memo to Grace Tully, his secretary, he wrote on October 18, 1943: "Take up with General Arnold and find out what is the latest date that I can deliver a Christmas tree to Winston Churchill and send it over by bomber or otherwise in order to reach him at Chequers, England, before Christmas. If I am away, tell Mr. Plog a week beforehand that it should be packed in burlap and sent to wherever General Arnold says. F.D.R." Two days later Tully wrote Plog, "The President wishes to send to the Prime Minister of Great Britain a Christmas tree. An Army truck will pick this tree up on December 11...."

Beginning with the 74th Congress in 1935, the rules for the convening of Congress were changed. The first session of each Congress now began in January (the first week after New Year's Day on off-years, the third week of January during presidential inaugural years). From Theodore Roosevelt's term on, each new Congress that began in the year a new president was sworn in was convened as late as May 19; in other years it continued to be convened on the first Monday in December, as set forth in the Constitution. With the change in the congressional calendar in 1935, the date of the presidential inauguration was also changed to coincide with the new schedule.

In a book published soon after her death, Eleanor Roosevelt recalled her many Christmases at the White House:

In Washington, ceremonies began on Christmas Eve. Franklin and I would greet our office people as they left, shaking hands with each one and wishing him a Merry Christmas.... My day had begun much earlier, with an appearance between nine and ten at one of the Washington theaters, where I gave

On October 3, 1863, President Lincoln proclaimed the first national Thanksgiving Day, setting aside the last Thursday in November for its observance. Thanksgiving was observed throughout the country on this day each year until 1939, when President Franklin Roosevelt moved it to the fourth Thursday of November, adding a week between Thanksgiving and Christmas that year. He had been persuaded by Fred Lazarus, Jr., president of Federated Department Stores, that a longer Christmas shopping season would help the economy. Within a few years most states had adopted the new date.

FDR's Christmas Turkey

The President loved the sight of a turkey. It had to come onto the table whole, so he could have the pleasure of carving, and the whole dinner was spoiled for him unless a necklace of little sausages was smoking all around the bird.... Chestnut was their favorite stuffing. For this I use two-day-old white or whole-wheat bread, never the crusts, cover them with water, let stand for five minutes, and squeeze it out. Crop the giblets fine, add two thirds of a cup of onions cooked until transparent in five tablespoons of fat, and thyme, parsley, savory, nutmeg, and salt. I stir the bread crumbs in with a two-tined fork, to keep the dressing light, then add the chestnuts that have been cooked and mashed through a sieve.

—Henrietta Nesbitt
White House Diary

out Christmas stockings to children gathered together by some civic groups. My next stop would be at the Volunteers of America, where baskets were being distributed to the needy, and I would give out a few of these and listen to some speeches and singing.

If the office party was at twelve o'clock, I had to hurry to get back to the White House and stand by the President during the reception. Then, immediately after lunch, there would be a Salvation Army party. After that, all of us, including the President, would get into the White House cars and go to the municipal tree-lighting ceremony, which was impressive, with lovely music. Then back to the White House, and at five o'clock, the President and I, his mother when she was alive, and any of the children who happened to be with us would receive the whole White House staff, with their families, in the East Room. Here, a handsome tree was set up in the east window, between the portraits of George and Martha Washington. It was always decorated completely in white and silver, and when the lights were lit, the toys for the children scattered under the tree, and the tables fanning out on either side laden with the older people's gifts, the scene was festive and beautiful.... After the party for the staff ... the little children had their supper while the big children decorated the family tree on the second floor. My husband would often start to read *A Christmas Carol* and would finish after dinner. Later in the evening, I always filled the Christmas stockings, which were hung in my husband's bedroom, and then attended church services, beginning at eleven-thirty. Getting to bed was a later affair, for every stocking had to be replaced exactly where each child or grandchild had hung it up.

In the morning, I got up early ... and dressed sufficiently to be presentable when the first grandchild would demand to go into 'Papa's' room ... then the littlest ones, sitting on his bed, would always empty their stockings.... My own children, most of them grown by this time, used to tease me about their stockings and say I took this opportunity to see that they were all equipped for cleanliness. Toothbrushes, soap, nail files were always somewhere in their stockings, and they took this laughingly.... [Then] we would all have breakfast in the West Hall....

Our own Christmas tree was not lighted until late in the afternoon of Christmas Day, because we went to church in the morning, and then there was lunch, and, for the President, work.

Christmas afternoon, I always make the rounds of Christmas trees in the alleys. The Alleys were some of the slums of Washington, and a group would set up sad little trees, around which children would gather for presents.... It was after five before our own Christmas-tree party began. We nearly always had as guests some friends as well as such family as could be mustered, and I would arrange piles of presents on chairs or even on the floor, always leaving some toys under the tree and handing these to Franklin to give to the children.

Franklin would be so interested in everyone else's presents that it might be four or five days after Christmas before we finally enticed him to open all his own gifts. Being an orderly person, I would always get mine opened before I went to bed, so I could prepare the list for thanking as soon as possible and get everything put away....

Christmas dinner always meant gathering together any of our family who lived in Washington.... After dinner, we usually had a movie, then everyone went home, with the feeling that Christmas had been well celebrated....

Despite these changes, some Washington traditions remained part of the old social calendar, including the Gridiron Club Dinner, which always held its annual jovialities and banquet before Christmas at the

Willard or some other big hotel. A white-tie roast given by members of the press since the 1890s for political celebrities, the event excluded women journalists and political wives. To correct this act of discrimination, Eleanor initiated the Gridiron Wives Dinner for three or four hundred Washington women professionals (and a few visiting celebrities), held on the same evening as the Gridiron. The Marine Band orchestra split into two units to serve both parties. One advantage of Eleanor's protest event was that she held hers at the White House.

Inevitably, the etiquette of addressing invitations for an afternoon tea and for an emancipated evening for the women of the press became tangled. Ruby A. Black, who ran an independent Washington news bureau and who later became a correspondent for UPI, sent a letter to the White House chief of protocol complaining that

there came a letter to 211½ Prince Street, Alexandria, an invitation to the "Gridiron Widows" party on December 21, addressed to "Mrs. Herbert Little." At that address live *Mr.* Herbert Little, who is my husband, Mrs. Nina Parten, who is my aunt, Miss Cornelia Jane Herbert Little, who is my 5-year-old daughter, and myself, whose name is Miss Ruby A. Black, at all times and under all circumstances.... It seems particularly strange that "Mrs. Herbert Little" should be invited to the "Gridiron Widows" party, since there is no such name on the Press Gallery list, the list of Mrs. Roosevelt's press conferences, or the Women's National Press Club list.

One unexceptional aspect of the White House during the Roosevelts' dozen years in residence was its food. When the president travelled to South America on the *Houston* just before Christmas, 1936, his housekeeper, Henrietta Nesbitt, provided the following list to the chief steward:

FOODS FOR THE PRESIDENT

Roast beef pink juice running

Steak either with mushrooms, fried onions, or
  Spanish sauce

Corned-beef hash with poached eggs

Lamb legs, filet mignon, or beef

Pork loin or crown, only once in a great while...

Chickens braised

Broilers plain or Maryland

Scrambled eggs, fried ham, bacon, or sausage for
  Sunday nights

Baked Virginia ham

Is fond of calf's liver, calf's kidneys, lamb kidneys,
  calf's brains, sweetbreads....

Foods sent by the public from all over the country were used in the White House kitchen to stretch the budget. According to Nesbitt, mangoes and frogs' legs were received from Florida, persimmons from California, and cantaloupes from the Middle West, as well as beef, ducks, quail, mountain sheep, moose, caribou, venison, brook trout, grouse, oysters, clams, smoked wild turkey, terrapin, and—the greatest prize of all—a big Nova Scotia salmon. For the Christmas season the featured attractions were the baked goods prepared in Henrietta's kitchen. Before Thanksgiving she began preparing plum puddings, which darkened by the day as they hung in the storeroom, white cakes, fruitcakes, mince pies, and pumpkin pies. Mrs. Roosevelt sent out "hundreds of boxes of [these] homemade things for the tables of friends."

For the Roosevelts and the whole country the watershed moment that separated a past filled with hope from a future consumed with trepidation occurred on December 7,

The highlight of each year's Gridiron Widows party was a skit performed by Eleanor, often accompanied by her best friend, Elinor Morgenthau, wife of the secretary of the treasury. In one, Eleanor presented a tableau vivant of "Whistler's Mother," which found its way into *Life* magazine.

Prime Minister Winston Churchill and President Roosevelt standing on the South Portico of the White House for the lighting of the National Community Christmas Tree, December 24, 1941, before a crowd of 15,000 gathered in the gloom. The Secret Service had requested that the tree-lighting ceremony and the Christmas tree, a possible air raid target, be eliminated, but Roosevelt objected. As a compromise, the tree was moved to the south grounds, just east of center. Only invited guests were permitted inside the gates; the rest of the crowd huddled in the darkness beyond the south fence. The Marine Band played Christmas music and ended the ceremonies with the "Star Spangled Banner" and "God Save the King."

1941, when Japanese planes attacked Pearl Harbor. During the next month the American nation was transformed. Old political rivalries melted away by Christmas, and a grand alliance was forged with Great Britain in a world war for freedom. A few days after the U.S. declaration of war Winston Churchill and his entourage left Whitehall, his London office, for a trip to Washington. He and his party arrived by ship at Hampton Roads on December 22 and flew into the new National Airport in Washington that night, where Roosevelt greeted them on the tarmac.

Churchill had first visited America in 1895 and again in 1900. Between these trips Churchill had served in the British army, fighting in the Sudan against 60,000 Dervishes in the last great cavalry charge in which lances were used. Arriving in New York in December 1900 for a lecture tour, he was first introduced by Mark Twain: "Mr. Churchill by his father is an Englishman, by his mother he is an American, no doubt a

blend that makes the perfect man. England and America; we are kin."

There was reason for Churchill to feel not entirely secure with his American ally that winter. England was having a terrible struggle getting help from the isolationist U.S. Congress. The U.S. ambassador to the Court of St. James, John Winant, was paid a salary of $17,500 a year, the same amount that Ambassador James Buchanan, who served in London in 1855, and Charles F. Adams, ambassador to Great Britain in 1861, were paid, a testament to England's declining prestige in America or the application of a very conservative compensation policy by the State Department.

But for the prime minister that Christmas of 1941 the binding ties of his American heritage seemed very strong indeed. In a Christmas Eve speech broadcast to America and the world at the lighting of the National Community Christmas Tree, he was eloquent. His brief message embraced the essence of the holidays, mingling patriotism, a sense of family togetherness, and the joys of the season into a single, sweeping idea:

I spend this anniversary and festival far from my country, far from my family, yet I cannot truthfully say that I feel far from home. Whether it be the ties of blood on my mother's side, or the friendships I have developed here over many years of active life, or the commanding sentiment of comradeship in the common cause of great peoples who speak the same language, who kneel at the same altars and, to a very large extent, pursue the same ideals, I cannot feel myself a stranger here in the centre and at the summit of the United States. I feel a sense of unity and fraternal association which, added to the kindness of your welcome, convinced me that I have the right to sit at your fireside and share your Christmas joys.

This is a strange Christmas Eve. Almost the whole world is locked in deadly struggle, and, with the most terrible weapons which science can devise, the nations advance upon each other. Ill would it be this Christmastide if we were not sure that no greed for the land or wealth of any other people, no vulgar ambition, no morbid lust for material gain at the expense of others, had led us to the field. Here, in the midst of war, raging and roaring over all the lands and seas, creeping nearer to our hearts and our homes, here, amid the tumult, we have tonight the peace of the spirit in each cottage home and in every generous heart. Therefore we may cast aside for this night at least the cares and dangers which beset us, and make for the children an evening of happiness in a world of storm. Here, then, for one night only, each home throughout the English-speaking world should be a brightly-lighted island of happiness and peace.

Let the children have their night of fun and laughter. Let the gifts of Father Christmas delight their play. Let us grown-ups share to the full in their unstinted pleasures before we turn again to the stern task and formidable years that lie before us, resolved that, by our sacrifice and daring, these same children shall not be robbed of their inheritance or denied their right to live in a free and decent world.

And so, in God's mercy, a happy Christmas to you all.

Churchill's words went beyond the season's greetings to remind Americans that their common values with the other English-speaking peoples of the world were encircled and defined by the spirit of Christmas. His conception of Christmas excluded the evil enemy, Hitler's Germany, and the untested ally of convenience, Joseph Stalin. That night Churchill's plea to merge Anglo-American forces into a single juggernaut struck precisely the right chord.

In the days that followed, Churchill's private talks with Roosevelt, Harry Hopkins, General Marshall, and others led to a unified command structure in Europe and the Pacific and a joint plan to fight the Germans in the north African desert. At the same time Roosevelt and Churchill used the public ceremonies during the holidays to further enhance the idea of a grand alliance.

On Christmas Day Churchill joined the presidential party for an interfaith service at Foundry Methodist Church, riding up 16th Street with Secret Service agents on the running boards. "I found peace in the simple service," said Churchill, "and enjoyed singing the well-known hymns, and one, 'O little town of Bethlehem,' I had never heard before." The following day he addressed an unusual holiday-week joint session of Congress, weaving the threads of the Atlantic Charter, a statement of mutual goals enunciated by himself and Roosevelt only four months before, into the whole cloth of British-U.S. collaboration. After taking a night train to Ottawa on December 28 and making a speech to the Canadian Parliament on the 30th, Churchill returned to Washington on New Year's Eve. The following day the entourage went to Christ Church in Alexandria, George Washington's house of worship. (Churchill, who loved the fact that his mother was American, could trace kinship with a Washington ancestor from his father's side of the family. He could also claim kinship with his host, Franklin Roosevelt, his seventh cousin once removed through Roosevelt's maternal grandmother's family.) After the service the party travelled to Mount Vernon, where Churchill placed a red, white, and blue wreath on Washington's tomb.

These public displays of solidarity and mutual devotion were one aspect of the consuming process of waging war. At appropriate moments the strategic participants paused for social meals with the Roosevelt household and their guests, who were many and frequent.

Given the secrecy in which Churchill crossed the Atlantic, not even Eleanor knew that he was coming for Christmas until he was practically on her doorstep, leaving her plans for the holidays in shambles. As it turned out, the only child at the White House for Christmas that year was Diana Hopkins, who lived at the White House with her father, Harry Hopkins, Roosevelt's chief aide. Luncheon and dinner guests who had been invited before the prime minister's arrival came along to mingle with Churchill, whose entourage included Lord Beaverbrook, his supply minister and publicist;

Lord Moran, his physician; and a variety of military specialists.

Having so many people under foot through the holidays was difficult. Churchill never seemed to sleep, leaving a trail of cigar smoke and ashes in his wake as he scurried about in his zippered jump suit between the Rose Bedroom, where he supposedly slept, to Hopkins's room, the Lincoln Bedroom across the hall, or to the map room, formerly the Monroe Room, down the hall. Fortunately, these haunts were all on the east side of the house, away from the family and the other house guests. On one occasion the prime minister received his visitors from the bathtub. He was known to order a large brandy at two and then four in the morning, calling for another with his morning breakfast tray and still another before noon. While the midnight oil burned in every corner of the White House that Christmas, security forces were busy erecting barriers and bunkers on the White House grounds, which were patrolled by machine gun–toting military policemen. Inside, the housekeeper, Henrietta Nesbitt was sewing black-out curtains while workers were painting the basement workroom windows black.

After church on Christmas Day the Roosevelts and Churchill were joined for lunch by the royal family of Norway, who were living in exile at Pook's Hill, a neighborhood in Bethesda, Maryland. In April 1940 they had been driven out of Oslo by Hitler's forces, who had installed a puppet prime minister, Vidkum Quisling, in their place. The party included the Crown Princess Martha, the Crown Prince Olav, their children, several other members of the royal family, the Hopkins family, and a few others.

"Wherever I Go" appeared as a Coca-Cola poster in 1943, providing a reminder at home that Coke, Americans, and Santa circled the globe. Especially in Thomas Nast's work, the symbols of Christmas became increasingly Americanized and secular. By the beginning of World War II Santa Claus had become a fixture in American advertising, in schools, and in the decoration of department store windows, city streets, and other public places. In 1931 the Coca-Cola Company had commissioned illustrator Haddon Sundblom to create an archetypical Santa that would be consistently recognized over time in a variety of situations. In previous years many Santas were dwarflike, following Clement Moore's 1822 description of Santa in "The Night Before Christmas" as "chubby and plump, a right jolly old elf." The Coca-Cola Santa soon became an all-American figure and was used as a model for other advertising and department store Santas.

By the time the dishes were cleared and the president and Churchill had retired to the map room, the usher's staff was resetting the table for 64 places, the largest Christmas dinner in White House history. The gathering at eight o'clock was a mix of family, friends, officials, and staff, including the Roosevelts' intimates, Harry and Elinor Morgenthau, Blaise and Betsy Mary de Sibour, Gordon and Janet Auchincloss, and Sunny and Sandy Forbes, along with Churchill, Beaverbrook, Admiral of the Fleet Sir Dudley Pound, Field Marshall Sir John Dill, and Roosevelts, Robinsons, and Delanos from both Franklin's and Eleanor's sides of the family.

While Churchill caused a certain degree of chaos, his visit relieved the household staff of the usual round of events that opened the social season, which had been suspended "for the duration." By New Year's Eve, with Churchill still on the train from Ottawa, the Roosevelts entertained quietly, inviting the Morgenthaus, Dr. Endicott Peabody, Bishop Julius Atwood, and a few others to dinner and a movie, *The Man Who Came to Dinner*.

Two weeks later Edith Helm, Eleanor Roosevelt's social secretary, walked into the second-floor sitting room and saw "a pile of gaily wrapped packages lying unopened.... President Roosevelt had not opened his Christmas gifts that fateful year."

CHAPTER ELEVEN

A Month of Christmases

When Christmas is spent outside one's own home, particularly in government surroundings such as the White House, you divide your Christmas into two parts. One covers your official obligations; the other, as far as possible, is the preservation of the home atmosphere and the home routine.

—Eleanor Roosevelt

In the final year of her life Eleanor Roosevelt remembered that White House Christmases were not so cheerful after 1941. Franklin's mother had died, the war continued, and the Roosevelt boys were scattered around the world in various theaters of battle. During the war years Christmas was nearly forgotten by the president as the first lady quietly filled her endless holiday gift lists. The 1944 holidays were probably the bleakest for the president, exhausted by the demands of the Allies' final offensive in Europe. Franklin Roosevelt died suddenly four months later, soon after his return from Yalta.

By 1945 the nation was completely obsessed by the events that brought the war to an end. "Not even Santa Claus," proclaimed *Time* magazine, "has been able to drive the bomb from the uppermost place in the U.S. mind."

After World War II Christmas and, indeed, life at the White House fundamentally changed. Family life, while hardly ever normal, became even more circumscribed and regimented as the public and press developed an insatiable hunger for details of the first family's lives. The informality of the Roosevelts' social life gave way to white tie and tails at state occasions as the United States assumed preeminent status among the nations of the world. For the Christmas holidays the White House became a place for public visitors and formal entertaining, planned and executed by an increasingly professional staff. For the Trumans and the next eight presidents, the atmosphere at the White House changed from Christmas celebrations that emphasized homemade treats and spontaneous family fun to those of an official observance, including more elaborate entertainments, lavish decorations on the State Floor, and an increase in the number of Christmas-oriented functions, leading the president and first lady into feverish rounds as party hosts before retiring,

Opposite: President Truman arrives home in Independence, Missouri, for the Christmas holidays, 1946.

exhausted, to some out-of-town retreat by Christmas Day. As the preparations became more complex and were cast on a grander scale, the work of setting up White House Christmases shifted from the first lady and her family to the increasingly important and burgeoning White House staff. As staffing at the household became more professional, the procedures became more institutionalized, often creating traditions that while seemingly time-honored had never actually existed before. Borrowing procedure and ceremonial flourishes from the British, the White House routine for state visits and special events has been cast as historical while, in fact, it is of modern invention. According to social historian Eric Hobsbawn, "Nothing appears more ancient, and linked to the immemorial past, than the pageantry which surrounds British monarchy in its public ceremonial manifestations. Yet . . . in its modern form it is the product of late nineteenth and twentieth centuries. Traditions which appear or claim to be old are often quite recent in origin and sometimes invented."

Political necessity, expediency, and serendipity have conspired in the evolution of White House ceremonies, particularly at Christmastime. In an earnest effort to produce historically founded surroundings and events, the first White House curator was detailed from the Smithsonian Institution in 1961, and a permanent White House Curator's Office was established in 1964 to document traditional protocols for ceremonial events in addition to its curatorial

HARRY S
AND
BESS WALLACE
TRUMAN
1945–53
✤

mandate. Consideration of history, precedent, and tradition at the White House, and the effort to create verisimilitude with the past, began in earnest during the Kennedy years. Since that time, substantial efforts have been made to incorporate into contemporary settings historically correct features—architectural details, furnishings, decoration and landscaping, and even the preparation of traditional recipes.

The orchestration of Christmas at the White House after World War II began to have similarities with that of a five-star hotel. From the Roosevelts' informality to the military correctness of the rites of the Truman and Eisenhower years, the story of Christmas at the White House has evolved into its present-day extravaganza, organized and executed by a battalion of staff members and consulting professionals.

Unlike the Roosevelts, who spent 10 of their 12 presidential Christmases in the White House, the Trumans went home to Missouri almost every year. In Independence Truman spent his first Christmas as president doing what he had done for years: eating three big Christmas dinners—at his 93-year-old mother's house; another at the home of his mother-in-law, Mrs. Madge Gates Wallace, who was 83; and a third at his aunt's, Margaret Truman Noland, who was 96. According to Margaret, the president's daughter, her father's two-day holiday jaunt to the Midwest in 1945 was very pleasant.

That year Truman waited until Christ-

Blair House—Temporary home of the President during the reconstruction of the White House 1948-1951

Christmas Greetings from the President and Mrs. Truman

1951

From Thanksgiving, 1948, to March 27, 1952, the Truman family resided at Blair House, across the street from the White House.

mas Day to leave Washington, a week later than Bess, Margaret, and Grandma Wallace. The weather in the capital was terrible; seven inches of snow had been dumped on the ground before the 25th. When Truman was ready to leave, a storm grounded the presidential plane, the *Sacred Cow*, for four hours before the impatient passenger ordered the plane aloft. According to Margaret Truman, "It was one of the wildest flights of his life."

Arriving in Independence after a 16-mile drive through sleet and snow from Kansas City Municipal Airport, Truman found that his wife and daughter would hardly speak to him. Margaret remembered that the "*New York Times*, the *Washington Post*, and other guardians of the republic castigated the President for 'taking chances with his personal safety.'" Bess's comments

when he got to 219 North Delaware Street were not much more cordial. To top off the holiday, the president received an urgent call from the White House the next day, informing him that the secretary of state, returning from a critical mission to Moscow, planned a "fireside chat" to the nation on his trip even before briefing the president. Truman rushed home on December 27. Having had some time to reflect, he wrote to his wife on December 28: "You can never appreciate what it means to come home as I did the other evening after doing at least one hundred things I didn't want to do and have the only person in the world whose approval and good opinion I value look at me like I'm something the cat dragged in."

The next year the first lady plunged into the social season wholeheartedly, returning the White House to the center of social entertaining after a moratorium of five years. Bess received women at back-to-back teas and evening receptions with Harry in formal attire. The round of events followed a nearly classic schedule. According to the records of Edith Helm, still the White House social secretary, the season began just after Thanksgiving and continued with a dozen white-tie state receptions and dinners.

Invitations to the receptions were increased from 1,000 to 2,000, while the diplomatic dinner had to be split into two events to accommodate everyone. In 1916, when Helm became social secretary for the Wilsons, there were only 35 chiefs of mission (ambassadors and ministers) in Washington. By 1946, after two world wars, the number had increased to 62, and the invitation list came to 200, counting wives, State Department officials, and White House staff. The big horseshoe table in the State Dining Room held 104. Helm remembered White House entertainments during the Truman years as "the very peak of social entertaining" in their formality, which contrasted with the informality of the Trumans' family life. In addition to the large, formal events, there were innumerable teas and receptions. On December 6, 1947, 2,500 members of the press were invited to a reception, with the president receiving until 10:30 p.m. There were two teas on the 11th and another two on the 13th. On the 15th the Duke and Duchess of Windsor came calling, while on the 24th the president dutifully pushed the button lighting the Christmas tree on the South Lawn to the accompaniment of a National Press Club Chorus rendition of "Go, Tell It on the Mountain."

Truman's address during the tree-lighting ceremony had a religious tone, incorporating Christian and patriotic themes:

In this great country of ours has been demonstrated the fundamental unity of Christianity and democracy.... We have our unique national heritage because of a common aspiration to be free and because of our purpose to achieve for ourselves and for our children the good things of life which the Christ declared He came to give all mankind.

Truman ended with the benediction, "Blessed are the peacemakers, for they shall be called the children of God."

The 1948 social season began with the official residence empty. The White House was "falling down, " as Truman recorded in his diary. A continuous stream of visitors for a century and a half had revealed the inadequacies of the structure's design. According to William Seale's detailed description of the demolition and rebuilding of the White House, "the immense rectangular box was cleaned of its historic insides ... a great hollow space some 85 feet north to south, 165 feet east to west, and 70 or 80 feet high." Anne Elizabeth Powell, writing in *Historic Preservation*, observed that "although care was taken to remove and place in storage much of the historic interior fabric, in the end most of this material...wound up on the caravan of trucks that for three weeks hauled White House 'debris' across the Potomac River to Fort Myer, Virginia, where it was used as landfill." The Trumans moved out of the White House before Thanksgiving, 1948, and did not return until March 27, 1952.

During the interim the White House functions were divided: the Trumans lived at Blair House, across the street, and the president worked at the Old Executive Office Building. Entertainments and receptions were held at the Carlton Hotel on 16th Street and at Blair House.

Ike was the first professional soldier since Grant and the last general to date (there had been nine others) to become president. Befitting the home of a military man, the Eisenhower White House—now a brand-new, air-conditioned modern residence inside—glistened like a shiny piece of reproduction period furniture. Mamie was so fastidious that she had porters brush away the footprints on the carpeting made by the porters doing the last-minute vacuuming before guests arrived. According to a Kennedy social secretary, Mary Thayer, white-tie events at the White House had "monotonously predictable guest lists. Mrs. Earl Warren, the wife of the Chief Justice, for instance, was the dinner partner of Vice-President Nixon for forty-two evenings during the Eisenhower Administration."

Mamie Geneva of Boone, Iowa, and later Denver, Colorado, was the second of four daughters of Min and John Doud, who at Christmas used to decorate their house and invite friends and neighbors over at the drop of a hat. The Douds celebrated Christmas enthusiastically, and Mamie brought her family's tradition into the White House, often dressing in holly berry red with white cuffs at family Christmas feasts. Each year

> **DWIGHT D. AND MAMIE DOUD EISENHOWER 1953–60**
> ✿

the decorations became more elaborate, reaching a peak of 27 decorated Christmas trees in 1958. Garlands of evergreens tied with big red ribbons festooned every window, and ropes of other greenery and red carnations encircled white columns. Green ribbons dangled from wall fixtures and mistletoe from chandeliers; red and white poinsettias filled every room.

For David Eisenhower, the president's grandson, and his two younger sisters, Barbara and Susan (Mary Jean, a third sister, was born in 1955), a White House Christmas was full of wonder. David recalled "a whole lot of activity downstairs, in the East Room, when I was small, and great feasts in the family dining room." His recollection did not extend to the incident, repeated by several members of the White House staff, when he woke the whole household as he crept downstairs to the East

Handmade Christmas card from David, Susan, and Barbara Eisenhower to Grandad, c. 1955.

The Eisenhowers' White House
Christmas card, 1955.

Season's Greetings
1955

Room at 3 a.m., "squealing with delight over the presents under the tree." According to David, "I have no recollection whatsoever that it ever happened."

The cozy, traditional Christmases of the Eisenhowers, who divided their holidays between the White House, the "Little White House," a cottage at the National Golf Club in Augusta, Georgia, and their farm in Gettysburg, Pennsylvania, were like those of the Trumans in many ways—completely unpretentious, quiet, and typical. There was, of course, the routine of official entertaining—no more and no less than before, except that greater emphasis was placed on military and international guests than earlier. Visitors at Christmas included the Shah of Iran and his queen one year and Madame Kasturbai Ghandi another year.

Unlike other presidents who distinguished political from household staff, the Eisenhowers brought both together, more than 500 people in all, for a Christmas party each year. For the personal staff, totalling perhaps two dozen, Mamie purchased gifts at Hecht's and Lansburgh's department stores, wrapping the packages herself to save money.

When the Eisenhowers had a night off from entertaining, they invariably had their dinner on trays in the third-floor solarium and watched television, a new pastime that instantly consumed the first family's and middle America's leisure time. During the day Mamie watched soap operas, but in the evenings she also enjoyed sitting with Ike, who loved the big variety shows. During the holiday week of their first year at the White

House, for example, they may have watched such specials as Bing Crosby with Louella Parsons singing "Adeste Fideles," Gian-Carlo Menotti's *Amahl and the Night Visitors* on the "Hallmark Hall of Fame," actress Lee Patrick reading *A Christmas Carol*, or other Christmas specials featuring Gary Moore, Donald O'Connor, and Gene Autry.

The most memorable moments of President Eisenhower's holidays occurred in 1960, during his last Christmas at the White House, when he and Mamie were already packing, making way for the Kennedys. Ike took the occasion of the lighting of the National Christmas tree, December 24, to address racial inequities in the United States:

We take great pride in our country's pre-eminent position in the family of nations. Yet, as we look into the mirror of conscience we see blots and blemishes that mar the picture of a nation of people who devoutly believe that they were created in the image of their Maker.

Too often we discern an apathy towards violations of laws and standards of private and public integrity. When, through bitter prejudice and because of differences in skin pigmentation, individuals cannot enjoy equality of political and economic opportunity we see another of these imperfections, one that is equally plain to those living beyond our borders. Wherever there is denied the right of anyone because he dares to live by the moral code to earn for himself and his family a living, this failure, too, is a blot on the brightness of America's image.

CHAPTER TWELVE

Christmas at Camelot

By 1961, with World War II a fading memory, the expanse of American energy and expertise spread to every corner of the globe. On Inauguration Day, a few weeks after their last White House Christmas, President and Mrs. Eisenhower were joined on the podium by the past and the future. The new first lady, Jacqueline Bouvier Kennedy, posed for photographers with Mrs. Eisenhower. Two future first ladies, Lady Bird Johnson and Betty Ford, were present, as were three former first ladies, Edith Wilson, Eleanor Roosevelt, and Bess Truman. All watched John F. Kennedy, the first Roman Catholic and the youngest man elected to the presidency, take the oath of office.

Ike was 63 years old and Mamie was 56 when they moved into the White House. John Kennedy was 43 and Jacqueline 31 when their time came. The two men could not have been more different in background and preparation for the presidency. From the beginning of Kennedy's term, differences between the two first ladies also rippled through the White House, as one generation of values and traditions was replaced by another.

JOHN F.
AND
JACQUELINE
BOUVIER
KENNEDY
1961–63
✤

Eisenhower, whose roots were in the Midwest, came to the presidency as a celebrated warrior. Kennedy, the son of a tycoon who produced whisky and movies, was groomed for power in urbane and sophisticated surroundings. Eisenhower was born in Texas, was raised in Kansas, and graduated from West Point. Kennedy was born in Massachusetts, was educated at Choate, Harvard, and Stanford, and served as secretary to his father, then U.S. ambassador to the Court of St. James. When he was 21 years old, he received a $1 million trust fund. Ike and Mamie married in Denver, Jack and Jacqueline at Newport. Ike's run for the presidency was his first attempt at elected office; his popularity as Allied commander catapulted him into office. Kennedy had been elected to the House of Representatives three times and the Senate twice and had once been a candidate for the vice presidential nomination before his bid for the White House in 1960.

The changes at the White House were evident in large and small ways. Mrs. Eisenhower used stationery purchased at Garfinckel's for her correspondence; her envelopes bore small return address stickers

Opposite: Christmas morning, 1961, Palm Beach, Florida. "The living room kind of looks like anybody's living room on Christmas morning," reported Pierre Salinger, the president's press secretary. Caroline was given a brown toy horse attached to a red surrey-tricycle, which she pedalled around the room.

sent to her by the Veterans of Foreign Wars that read "Mrs. Dwight D. Eisenhower, 1600 Pennsylvania Avenue, Washington, 6, D.C." For her correspondence Mrs. Kennedy used a heavy vellum engraved stock. After the White House renovation by the Trumans, the Eisenhowers lived comfortably among the chintz and reproduction furniture from B. Altman's. For Mrs. Kennedy, who grew up among heirloom pieces gracing residences in the gold coasts of the Hamptons and Newport, redecorating the White House was a pressing priority.

As Jacqueline Kennedy transformed the Green and Red rooms and then the Blue Room into parlors in which every piece of furniture was steeped in history, she also very quickly transformed the place of the White House in the public's consciousness and understanding. The redecoration of the

Red Room was centered on American furniture in the Empire style of 1830–50, while the Blue Room was decorated to reflect its life during Monroe's administration, when furniture for the White House was imported from France.

With the newly acquired antiques and period-sensitive decoration came professionalism in presentation, a more imaginative orchestration of dinners, social entertainments, and receptions, and a deliberate shift away from some of the more arcane and inconvenient traditions of protocol and etiquette. This skillful updating replaced the "traditional stuffed shirt" with "gaiety, informality and culture," according to one British journalist. Although social secretaries such as Belle Hagner, who had served Theodore and Edith Roosevelt, and Edith Helm, who had worked for the Wilsons, Roosevelts, and Trumans, had cer-

Caroline plays with a friend in front of a 16-foot-tall Christmas tree in the Main Foyer, 1962, decorated according to a *Nutcracker Suite* theme. The Blue Room was undergoing renovation at the time. The White House was decorated in the style of an American country house, with a dozen unadorned trees, garlands, greens, and masses of holly festooned throughout the State rooms.

tainly been professionals, their domain was defined by strict rules that were rarely broken or even questioned. Mrs. Kennedy abandoned the entire formal social season of state occasions for 1961 and reshaped it the next year to combine many traditional events that had stood the test of time at the White House.

The Kennedys modified the guest lists and the routine—the music, food, and regi-men for receiving—and changed the dress code from white tie to black tie. At one 1961 event Adam Clayton Powell discussed Caribbean politics with Pablo Casals, as Leonard Bernstein found common ground with Andrew Wyeth, Charles Lindbergh, and Geraldine Page over canapés and cocktails in the Red Room before moving on to the State Dining Room for dinner. After dessert Isaac Stern played in the East Room while Tennessee Williams and Arthur Miller continued their conversation in a whisper from the back row. If there was no musicale, men and women would actually remain together for the rest of the evening, rather than the men going to the Green Room for cigars and port and the women to the Red Room for coffee and liqueurs as they did during the Eisenhower administration.

Although the sagging timbers beneath the White House floors were replaced during the Truman years, the staff continued to tread along well-worn paths for some time, following rituals and a way of life that reached across the tenancies of more than 30 families and 15 decades. When the Eisenhowers moved into what was essentially a new house, they did their best to maintain the kind of tradition that is practiced by the military, a tradition closely bounded by precedence. The style of the Kennedy White House evolved beyond the first lady's personal preferences into what was an essentially new tradition, with major and minor elaborations that continue even today.

The trend began after World War II, when increased attention to the presidency by the world's press and the introduction of television news eliminated what was left of the first family's privacy. The comfortable, familiar Christmas traditions of the Truman family remained in Independence, Missouri, where they celebrated the holiday, partly because of the complete dishabille of the White House. Since a golf course could not be accommodated on the White House grounds, Eisenhower preferred Augusta to Washington for his Christmas holidays. By the time Kennedy came to office, the personal connection between the White House

and its occupants at Christmastime had been practically eliminated. Under Kennedy the staff size and housekeeping budgets grew enormously, creating a new middle management. Everything else grew proportionately. Indeed, everyday life at the White House, which had been made modest by Franklin and Eleanor Roosevelt (and had been kept that way by the Trumans and Eisenhowers) was suddenly redefined in the tradition of Theodore and Edith Roosevelt.

The assembly of antiques, redecoration of walls, and acquisition of paintings invigorated the nearly new house with mostly old adornments, creating the illusion of ancient venerableness. The affluence of the 1960s also helped change the image of White House decor from dull dowdiness to recherché elegance. In time, this metamorphosis has become an important facet of White House life, as successive families live among 18th-century heirlooms housed in the rarified atmosphere of a museum.

Given the focus on the Kennedys' élan, the changes in staffing and planning, procedures, budget, security, communications, and precision of White House operations were barely noticed by the public. At the beginning events were simply bigger. At the Kennedys' 1962 Christmas party for the staff, more than 1,200 people attended, more than double the number who attended the Eisenhowers' last staff party, reflecting a doubling of the White House staff in only two years. After the redecoration Mrs. Kennedy brought millions of Americans into "her" home through a television special that created widespread interest in the activities at the president's residence. This publicity and its ripple effects created a magnification of the White House that soon translated into a heightened awareness of American style and culture around the world, thus opening markets for American goods and services, particularly movies, music, architecture, and art. Among journalists, public officials, movie stars, and artists of all kinds, the White House became a mecca of refined sensibilities and gracious living. In the eyes of world leaders the American presidency had finally arrived at a style that was both original and admirable, a blend of studied simplicity and the brash spontaneity for which Americans were known; in combining efficiency and lavishness, it reflected a standard set by American business to the world.

For the Kennedys Christmas was simply part of their joie de vivre, no more or less important for entertaining than other seasonal opportunities. Heads of state from every part of the world sought White House invitations for Washington visits. Sixty-six heads of state were entertained by the Kennedys while they lived at the White House, more than double the number of state dinners given by any single previous administration.

As the pace of entertaining quickened, expenses escalated. At every turn housekeeper Anne Lincoln had to find ways to economize. During the Eisenhowers' residency, liquor for parties came from bootleg caches confiscated by treasury agents. By 1961 procedures were tightened and the practice was abandoned, forcing the White House to shop for the best prices at local retail liquor stores. The wine and spirits order for a typical state dinner held that winter included nine cases of Dom

Pérignon, another nine cases of a good white California chablis, two cases each of Cutty Sark scotch and Old Grand-Dad bourbon, and a case of Beefeater gin. Whatever the amount (which was borne by the State Department when official foreign visitors were entertained), the cost was not a high priority in menu planning. For one important head of state, 180 guests sat down to baby lobsters and Roquefort mousse (which required 20 pounds of cheese), pâté de foie gras, filet mignon, and strawberries Romanoff (which required 90 pints of berries and 22 quarts of whipping cream).

The excitement the Kennedys inspired often became frenzy, and their popularity soared. By midterm, social secretary Tish Baldrige, a veteran foreign service officer and experienced manager, buried beneath a flurry of phone messages and memoranda most of the time, left her job to take a calmer position with Joseph Kennedy's Chicago Merchandise Mart (although she returned as a consultant to First Lady Nancy Reagan two decades later). She was replaced by Nancy Tuckerman, the first lady's prep school roommate. After a nonstop, frantic two years the East Wing finally had a respite when Mrs. Kennedy curtailed her activities because of her pregnancy.

During the two holiday seasons that they were in residence at the White House, the Kennedys stayed at the home of C. Michael Paul, a family friend, in Palm Beach, Florida, a mile down the beach from the home of Joseph Kennedy. The president's father had been incapacitated by a stroke in December 1961, just before the family arrived, casting a pall over their holiday celebrations. On a rainy Christmas morning four-year-old Caroline and one-year-old John, Jr., opened their presents, assisted by Luella Hennessey, the children's nurse. Afterward, the family visited the elder Kennedy at St. Mary's Hospital and took communion at a chapel on the hospital grounds. A Christmas dinner of turkey and mince pie was served later in the day,

attended by the president and his family, including Edward and Joan Kennedy, Peter and Patricia Lawford, and Prince and Princess Radziwell. The president's mother, Rose, remained at the hospital.

The next Christmas was brighter. The president's children rose with the sun, and the temperature reached the low eighties by afternoon, when the family took a sailing excursion on their yacht, the *Honey Fitz*.

Before leaving for Florida, the first family hosted only three parties specifically related to Christmas, including one for the staff, one for the children of diplomats, and one for underprivileged children. At each event the Kennedys' two children, Caroline and John, Jr., were whisked in and out, closely shielded from the public eye by their protective mother.

At the 1961 staff party the Red Room was opened for the first time since its redecoration. Fires blazed in all the fireplaces as the president and first lady strolled through the state rooms, greeting their guests. The Marine Orchestra, divided between the East

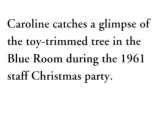

Caroline catches a glimpse of the toy-trimmed tree in the Blue Room during the 1961 staff Christmas party.

Room and the State Dining Room, played a program featuring "O Come, All Ye Faithful," "Silent Night, Holy Night," "Glory to God in the Highest," and "Thou Child Divine." Eggnog, fruit punch, and Christmas cookies in the shape of Santas and trees were served.

Even the most simple of ceremonies could become complex when orchestrated by the Kennedy White House, as illustrated by the correspondence that led to the lighting of the National Community Christmas Tree in 1962. On November 5 Edward Carr, president of the Christmas Pageant of Peace, wrote a long letter to Jack McNally, special assistant to the president, seeking a firm date between December 19 and 23 for the president's lighting of the tree. He reminded McNally that invitations had to be printed and mailed, arrangements for television time had to be made, a program had to be printed, and arrangements for video tape had to be made so that the ceremony could be broadcast via Telstar to the world on Christmas Eve. In addition, an October 11 letter from the national president of the Jaycees was attached, requesting that similar but smaller Pageants for Peace and tree lightings be staged at state capitals around the country at the same moment that the tree was lighted in Washington. Finally, Carr reminded McNally of "all of the many hundreds of people connected with this program [who] will deeply appreciate your assistance."

Before Thanksgiving McNally sent a memorandum to Ken O'Donnell about the Carr letter, and December 18 was set as the date for the tree lighting. Having his response, the pageant staff sent out invitations to thousands of people in the Washington, D. C., area:

The President of the United States
will light
The National Community Christmas Tree
at five o'clock
on Tuesday, December the eighteenth
In the President's Park
South of the White House
The Committee
requests the honor of your presence at
this ceremony opening The Christmas Pageant of
Peace
Please reply on enclosed card before December eight
The ceremony begins
at four-thirty o'clock

Enclosed was a second invitation to an evening of traditional music and dance at Lisner Auditorium and response card and envelope.

Despite all these preparations and pleas for a firm date, only a few days before the event, the White House changed the time and date to December 17 at five o'clock, causing the pageant committee to send notices to all the invitees and accelerate the arrangements by 24 hours. As it turned out, the president left Washington on December 14 without lighting the tree, leaving the honors to the vice president three days later.

The last event of the Kennedy White House was a belated birthday party for Caroline and John, Jr., on December 5, 1963, the day before they left the residence. In the shadow of their father's assassination in Dallas, Kennedy cousins and a few playmates gathered to celebrate the children's November birthdays in a private event in the residence, which was not yet decorated for Christmas.

CHAPTER THIRTEEN

The Gilded Cage

Of six Christmas Days during Lyndon Johnson's tenure as president, four were spent at the LBJ Ranch in Johnson City, Texas. During all except their first White House Christmas, the first family's schedule was packed with holiday events in Washington from the first of December to the first of January. The Johnsons' most consequential Christmas at the White House was 1967, when their daughter Lynda was married.

By the mid-1960s the traditional social season, which had begun with Abigail Adams's first New Year's levee in 1801 and had evolved to a series of formal dinners and receptions through the mid-20th century, had succumbed to a more sophisticated capital that saw a less rigid, more creative form of entertaining during the holidays. December events at the White House became more focussed on Christmas. The de rigueur diplomatic reception that opened the season for more than a century was now transformed into a party for the children of diplomats, often with clowns and balloons among the Christmas tinsel and gingerbread. Although the traditional opening events were gone, the formalities of state

LYNDON B.
AND
LADY BIRD TAYLOR
JOHNSON
1963–69
✿

occasions remained when foreign dignitaries came calling, an increasingly frequent event.

While Kennedy learned the legislative ropes from Johnson, LBJ and Lady Bird reaped the benefits of the new status brought to the presidency by the suave young president and his first lady. The new rules were that there were no rules, simply large measures of common sense blended with an awareness of history and tradition and loads of savoir faire. The challenge for the Johnsons was to build on the Kennedy legacy while creating a niche of their own. The White House of John Kennedy's gilded age became, in many ways, Lyndon Johnson's gilded cage. For Johnson, following in the wake of the Kennedy assassination and soon finding himself mired in Vietnam, the road to glory was strewn with obstacles. Despite the political problems, the Johnsons entertained constantly and brilliantly, a testament to their Washington experience, Mrs. Johnson's extraordinary abilities, and her husband's irrepressible sociability. For the first time at White House receptions women were kissed in the receiving line; there was dancing at every state dinner, with charming Lyndon changing partners at

Opposite: Lynda Bird Johnson and Charles Robb pass under a saber arch at their White House wedding, December 9, 1967.

Johnson family Christmas during the Vietnam War, December 24, 1968. From left: Luci Baines Nugent, Patrick Lyndon Nugent, Mrs. Johnson, President Johnson, Lynda Bird Robb, and Lucinda Desha Robb.

every turn. Johnson also ordered photographs by the thousands, keepsakes that thrilled and flattered his guests.

In his first year in the White House, as Johnson campaigned for a term of his own, his theme was the "Great Society," which focused on fairness and equal opportunity for African Americans and provided, finally, a moral framework for increased prestige among the other nations of the world. The immense interest in the White House and the presidency created by the Kennedys continued with the Johnsons until midterm, when events in Southeast Asia began to dampen the petticoat swirl of the Johnsons' Texas-style parties.

Like Truman and Roosevelt and unlike Hoover, Eisenhower, and Kennedy, the Johnsons had a family homestead deeply rooted in a community—Johnson City, Texas. Down-home events were a mainstay of the Johnson style of entertaining. The first social event of Johnson's presidency was a barbeque held at the LBJ Ranch for Ludwig Erhard, chancellor of the Federal

Republic of Germany, on December 29, 1963, a few days after the official 30-day mourning period for John Kennedy had ended. Johnson had met Erhard at the Kennedy funeral in Washington in November and had invited him to return the following month. Although a few White House staff and State Department officials were in attendance, the guest list featured more than a hundred Texans, the closest hometown friends of the Johnsons. Not a single member of Congress had been invited, although a score of Texas officials drove over for a plate of roasted pork and cole slaw. Because of bad weather, the event was moved to the Stonewall High School gymnasium, providing from the start a sharp contrast to Harry Truman's white-tie receptions or Jacqueline Kennedy's continental cuisine for distinguished foreign visitors.

The number of heads of state who visited during the next two years was impressive, and the Christmas season was the premier period for entertaining. For the Johnsons these state visits were a natural opportunity to entertain with traditional elegance at the White House, without self-consciousness or criticism from the press. Given the new sensibility toward discrimination, the disadvantaged, and the displaced, the Johnsons were careful not to appear to be elitists.

The cycle of visits from British and British colony dignitaries during the Christmas holidays that had begun during World War II continued. In addition, visits of German officials increased, perhaps an acknowledgment of American ties to these cultures at Christmastime.

Before the era of jet transport, visits by

heads of state to the White House were infrequent. Indeed, between 1789 and 1925 only 13 heads of state were entertained by U.S. presidents, and only about a dozen more between the Teapot Dome scandal and Pearl Harbor. Churchill and William MacKenzie King, prime minister of Canada, had attended White House meetings during Christmas, 1941, and the British and Canadian prime ministers visited again around the holidays in 1942, 1943, and 1945. Prime Minister Clement Attlee was a guest at the White House in December 1950, Prime Minister Robert Gordon Menzies of Australia in 1952, and Churchill again in 1953, and Prime Minister Jawaharlal Nehru from India visited the Eisenhowers in Gettysburg in 1956. Erhard came again during the Christmas season in 1965. Prime Minister Harold Wilson visited during the holidays in 1964, and his successor, Edward Heath, visited from December 17 to 18, 1970, and again from December 12 to 18, 1971. In December 1974 Pierre Trudeau of Canada visited the Fords, followed the same week by Chancellor Helmut Schmidt of the Federal Republic of Germany. The record of Anglo-American meetings during the holidays is more striking when instances of travel by U.S. presidents during the holiday season are also considered. Woodrow Wilson dined at Buckingham palace during Christmas week, 1918, with George V and Prime Minister Lloyd George; Eisenhower met with Churchill in Bermuda on December 8, 1953; Kennedy visited Harold MacMillan in Bermuda from December 21 to 22, 1961, and in Nassau from December 18 to 21, 1962. Lyndon Johnson visited Australia from December

21 to 22, 1967, and Nixon travelled to Bermuda to confer with Prime Minister Heath from December 20 to 21, 1971, after also spending a weekend with him at Camp David. In recent years the pattern has changed somewhat, although some of Ronald Reagan's meetings with Margaret Thatcher and George Bush's meetings with John Major have taken place over the holidays.

When Chancellor Erhard returned to the United States in 1965, the Johnsons rolled out the red carpet at the White House. Liz Carpenter, Mrs. Johnson's press secretary, issued a release stressing the Christmas theme:

Christmas caroling—old and new—will be the feature of the dinner tonight honoring His Excellency Dr. Ludwig Erhard, Chancellor of the Federal Republic of Germany.

The Chancellor will be welcomed to the White House dinner at eight o'clock by sixty American Light Opera Company carolers, on the steps of the south portico. They will sing familiar carols.

During dinner, there will be strolling carolers in the State Dining Room—the University of Maryland's Madrigal Singers, who will present 16th- and 17th century carols in English. They will be dressed in colorful Renaissance costumes.

After-dinner entertainment will highlight Robert Merrill, who this year marks his twentieth anniversary as one of the great stars of the Metropolitan Opera Company.

Mr. Merrill, accompanied by his wife, will sing Christmas songs—both American and German.... The Madrigal singers will present three 16th and 17th-century German Christmas carols.

There will be 140 guests at dinner, seated at tables of ten. Some additional guests will come in after dinner for the Christmas entertainment. The

State dinner for Prime Minister Harold Wilson, hosted by President and Mrs. Johnson, December 7, 1964.

RUFFLES AND FLOURISHES

On December 7, 1964, Prime Minister Wilson visited the Johnsons at the White House, receiving full state honors upon his arrival. Although these White House arrival ceremonies varied somewhat according to the season, weather, and stature of the guest, the routine has remained much the same for many years. Every step is orchestrated at these events. A briefing paper on the arrangements for the Wilson arrival at the South Lawn of the White House included these details:

At 11:10 a.m. the President and Mrs. Johnson will depart from the President's office in the White House. The trumpets will play four ruffles and flourishes and "Hail to the Chief." During the playing of "Hail to the Chief" the President and Mrs. Johnson will walk to the vicinity of the platform to await the arrival of the Prime Minister of the United Kingdom.

At 11:15 a.m. Prime Minster Wilson, accompanied by Ambassador [Angier Biddle] Duke, and his party will enter the Southwest Gate of the White House. The trumpets will sound a fanfare as the cars approach ... the Prime Minister's car will stop at the Diplomatic Entrance where Ambassador Duke will present the Prime Minister to President and Mrs. Johnson. Then

Secretary Rusk and General Wheeler will be introduced.... Following photographs, the President and Mrs. Johnson will escort the Prime Minister onto the platform. When all are in position, the Commander of Troops will bring the Honor Guard to Present Arms.

As the Commander of Troops salutes, the trumpets will sound four ruffles and the band will play the national anthem of the United Kingdom, followed by the national anthem of the United States. The 19-gun salute will be fired simultaneously with the music.

Upon completion of honors, the troops will be given Order Arms, the Commander will salute and report, "Sir, the Honor Guard is formed."

President Johnson will escort the Prime Minister toward the band. The Commander of Troops will take a position to the right of the Prime Minister and guide him through the inspection. As the inspection party turns in front of the band, President Johnson will take a position to the right of the Commander of Troops.

The memorandum continues, step by step, through the inspection, return to the platform, presentation of remarks, alternative arrangements for inclement weather, car seating arrangements, maps and layouts of the scene, and a complete listing of the welcoming committee.

U.S. Marine Band will play for the arrival of guests and for special dinner music.

The menu consists of Lobster Imperial, Roast duckling, Lettuce salad with Brie Cheese, and for dessert, a yule log—a chocolate cake frosted with mocca butter.

Flowers adorning the tables will include purple and lavender stock and Anemone, lavender heather, pompom chrysanthemums, white stevia, red roses, marguerite daisies, and podocarpus foliage.

There will be Christmas bouquets throughout the house, in addition to the large early American tree in the center of the Blue Room. Small Christmas trees, decked with tinsel and popcorn, are used throughout the mansion as well. The mantels of fireplaces will be decked in holly and Christmas greens....

Mrs. Johnson's gown is a statuesque deep American beauty red silk fabric....

While social secretary Bess Abell and her staff were busy with the Erhard state dinner, they also had to plan for two luncheons—one for British Prime Minister Harold Wilson and one for his wife—to be held simultaneously at 1 p.m. on December 17, three days before the state dinner. Attached to the suggested guest list was a memo from the protocol office to Bess Abell:

Subject: Standby Gift for the Rt. Hon. Harold Wilson, O.B.E., M.P., Prime Minister of the U.K. and Mrs. Wilson.

Mr. Judd [U.K. desk officer] maintains that a firm decision has been reached that there will be <u>no</u> gifts. However, he went on to say that the last time this was agreed upon, Prime Minister Wilson did indeed give gifts to the President which was somewhat embarrassing as he had nothing to return.

Therefore, Mr. Judd feels that a "standby" gift should be in the president's office which he may or may not give according to the circumstances (e.g. if P.M. Wilson gives him something, he will present it, or if the "mood" is such that he wishes to do so, he will have it there for that purpose).

He said that P.M. Wilson already had an official photograph. What about the family one?

I enclose herewith a little sea chest (cigar box) which I feel would be "ideal" for a "standby" gift....

The wedding of Lynda Bird Johnson and Charles S. Robb, a captain in the U.S. Marines, in the East Room on December 9, 1967, was planned with military precision, perfect timing, dramatic ceremony, and extraordinary preparations by the usher's office, the social secretary, and the first family. Fundamental to its success was the even flow of people and events from the first moment, 2 p.m., when various members of the wedding party were directed to present themselves at the East Gate in time to dress for the wedding, through to 6:30 p.m., when the scenario from Bess Abell's office indicated that "three aides ... prepared to clear sufficient space in the East Room after the cake cutting so that members of the receiving line and wedding party can dance the traditional waltzes." Some 650 people attended the wedding. As many as two dozen military aides were scattered around the White House to direct

Admission card (top) and parking card for the Johnson-Robb wedding, December 9, 1967.

The Engelhard crèche was first unveiled in the East Room, December 15, 1967.

people and keep order, each linked by small, unobtrusive walkie-talkies with Abell and her two assistants on the ground floor, state floor, and upstairs. The key moment of the event came at 3:45 p.m., when the groom and his best man descended the third floor by elevator to the State Floor and proceeded concealed (all the rooms— the State Dining Room and the Red, Blue, and Green rooms—were closed) to their waiting positions in the Green Room. At the same time the six sword-bearers moved to the Blue Room, and the ushers moved into position in preparation for the bride's descent of the Grand Staircase. At exactly 4 p.m., Abell gave the signal, and the brides-maids and wedding party descended the Grand Staircase to the pop of strobe lights and flash bulbs of photographers at the foot of the stairs. At the conclusion of the ceremony, the swordsmen, waiting in the Blue Room, marched into the Cross Hall to the entrance of the East Room and formed a saber arch, under which the bride and groom and then the rest of the wedding party passed.

The frenzy of events surrounding the Johnson-Robb Christmas nuptials gave way to more routine social functions characteristic of any administration. There was, of course, Mrs. Johnson's oversight of the White House Christmas decorations and the rounds of official duties as hostess for a multitude of holiday events.

Mrs. Johnson also continued her involvement with the Committee for the Preservation of the White House, established during the Kennedy administration, and presided over numerous events such as the presentation of the Presidential Medal

of Freedom, luncheons for the National Council on the Arts (the forerunner of the National Endowment for the Arts), and, in later years, the Kennedy Center Honors. Through such activities she developed friendships with a number of philanthropists who later took an active interest in the president's and first lady's cultural initiatives. Patrons such as Joseph Hirshhorn, Armand Hammer, Carol Hausmann, Henry Dupont, and Jane Engelhard became important to Mrs. Johnson's projects. For some, the effort extended well beyond writing checks or donating a piece of furniture or a painting.

Jane and Charles Engelhard, who later made a substantial contribution to building the diplomatic reception rooms at the State Department, provided an antique crèche as a gift to the White House during the Christmas season of 1967, just after the Johnson-Robb wedding. Mrs. Engelhard was on the Committee for the Preservation of the White House and saw a great need for special White House decorations. The story of the White House crèche provides a perspective on serious philanthropy and the coordination of efforts between the White House and patrons with the means, taste, and time to help out.

During the Kennedys' first White House Christmas, the first lady borrowed an antique crèche from Loretta Howard of New York for display in the East Room, a loan that continued until 1964, when the crèche was donated to the Metropolitan Museum of Art. After some discussion with Mrs. Johnson during the Christmas season of 1966, Jane Engelhard began to assemble information relating to the purchase and gift of an antique crèche. She visited Thomas Hoving and Arthur Houghton at the Metropolitan Museum, who informed her that the largest collection of crèches in the world was at the Bayerischen National-museum in Munich. She also discovered that there was an American Christmas Crib Society and that an International Crib Congress had been held in Rome in 1954 and in Barcelona in 1957. In a letter to Mrs. Johnson, Engelhard reported that there was a mechanical infant Jesus at the Musée Borély in Marseilles "which claps its hands when an important personage enters, or, alternatively it can outstretch its arms. I am sure this would appeal to the President, but I am not promising anything as exciting as this."

After getting the dimensions for the East Room stage and other particulars and discussing the project with a New York set designer, Engelhard set off for Europe to find a crèche. Her report of the trip describes meetings at the Bayerischen Nationalmuseum in Munich and in Rome with Angelo Stefanucci, a world expert and the president of the Italian Christmas Crib Association. After visits to various antique dealers, she found 18th-century crib figures and a nativity crib offered by Marisa Capel-lo Piccoli from Naples. The report was extensive, including a bibliography and details of each of her meetings. After due consideration, she secured 20 figures plus animals and miniature objects, "as magnifi-cent as you could find in any museum." She

enclosed a letter to the U.S. ambassador to Italy, describing the purchase and requesting help in obtaining a license from the Italian government to export the figures to the United States.

In a press release issued by Liz Carpen-ter, the crèche was described as a "Nativity scene, [containing] thirty baroque carved figures including the Holy Family, the three kings and their attendants, shepherds, angels, cherubs, and various animals associ-ated with the manger scene. Brightly col-ored and richly clothed, the figures range from 12 to 18 inches high and are delicately carved in wood." On December 15, 1967, the crèche was unveiled in the East Room, dramatically staged and lighted by set designer Donald Oenslager. A reception for Engelhard was held afterward in the Blue Room, with the Johnsons and Engelhards posed next to the Christmas tree to receive guests. In 1978 Engelhard purchased 10 more antique figures, and a new set was designed by Loretta Howard.

In Drew Pearson's syndicated column of December 29, 1968, he noted that Christ-mas at the White House for the Johnsons was "not as gay this year as last. 'We came into the White House four and we're going out eight,' said Mrs. Johnson [her two daughters, Lynda Bird and Luci Baines, had each married and produced a grandchild—Patrick Lyndon Nugent and Lucinda Desha Robb]. Two of the eight, however, were in Vietnam, casting a shadow over the celebra-tion."

CHAPTER FOURTEEN

Molding Tradition

The Johnsons, Nixons, and Fords all had daughters of dating age when they entered the White House. The Johnson girls both married men from the Midwest who served in the military during the Vietnam era. The husbands of the Nixon daughters came from socially and politically prominent families from the Northeast. Tricia married Edward Cox, who hailed from the patrician Livingston family of New York. They were married in 1971 in the first outdoor wedding in White House history. Julie, who was two years younger, had married during her Christmas vacation from college, after her father's election but before he took office in 1968. Susan Ford married at age 21, two years after leaving the White House.

For each of these young women the passage from childhood to adulthood was stilted, as Secret Service agents, journalists, groupies, and political aides tagged along on dates, appeared at parties, and generally cramped the style of even the most suave suitors or friends. During their growing-up years, 1964–76, much of American youth was enamored of marijuana, civil disobedi-

RICHARD M.
AND
PATRICIA RYAN
NIXON
1969–74
❁

ence, and rock and roll. At the same time the role of women in society underwent a profound change. Within this maelstrom these White House daughters, all of them with previous Washington experience as the sometime hostesses of vice presidents, were set above the fray, isolated from all but a few of their peers.

For Julie and David Eisenhower, who grew up knowing each another (both were four years old when Julie's father became vice president and David's grandfather became president) and had made the decision to marry a month before the Nixons moved into the White House, the problems were somewhat different. They were married in a private ceremony in New York City on December 22, 1969, by Dr. Norman Vincent Peale. Ike and Mamie, who were both hospitalized at Walter Reed Hospital in Washington, D.C., watched the ceremony via a closed-circuit television hook-up provided by NBC. After the ceremony the couple flew to Palm Beach, Florida, for their honeymoon, surprising the Nixons, who were vacationing at their new house on Biscayne Bay, with a Christmas Day visit. In a humorous account by Julie, the evening

Opposite: Pat Nixon with Big Bird during a Christmas party for the children of diplomats, December 22, 1970.

presented an almost-typical family tableau: The house was sparsely furnished and my parents and Tricia were practically camping out. My father decided that an after-Christmas-dinner fire would end the day in a fitting manner. Manolo [the butler] somehow scrounged up wood, crumpled newspapers, and struck a match. The fire blazed up nicely. Then smoke slowly, steadily filled the room. We were watching a movie on television, and my father kept repeating, as if to reassure himself, "Isn't this wonderful? Isn't this fun having a fire and being here together?" Meanwhile, our eyes were killing us, and it was getting harder and harder to breathe. The flue was open, but I do not think the fireplace had ever been used and it obviously didn't work.

Mother was the first to slip out quietly. As the smoke got worse my father, only slightly less enthusiastic, repeated again, "Isn't it fun to have a fire?" David lay down on the floor next to the dogs, who had stretched out very low in order to breathe more easily, but within minutes, Pasha and Vicky got up and staggered out of the room. Finally my father

was the only one left. Manolo and several Secret Service agents moved in and put out the fire.

Many years later Mrs. Nixon remembered the time as her favorite Christmas. Julie remembered it as a time when the astronauts of Apollo 8, the first men to circle the moon, read from Genesis 1:1 and Clement Moore's "Twas the Night Before Christmas."

Julie's Christmas memories date more from her childhood than from the period when her parents lived in the White House. "Dad was very sentimental about Christmas, " she said. "I guess it was because he had so little as a child. He was almost childlike about presents." David recalled that the Christmas ambiance at the Nixon White House was "spare" compared to the opulent decorations in the East Room and upstairs West Hall when the Eisenhowers were in residence. "Nixon's was a wartime era," he offered. "The other [the Eisenhower admin-

First Lady Pat Nixon and Julie Nixon Eisenhower help decorate the State Floor, 1971.

Nixon family dinner in the Red Room, December 25, 1970. Seated clockwise: Mamie Eisenhower, President Nixon, Trisha, Julie, Mrs. Nixon, David Eisenhower.

Opposite: The Nixons inspect a snowman built by the White House staff, December 17, 1973.

The first candlelight tour of the White House, December 27, 1971. The Marine Band plays in the entrance hall.

istration] was not. It was a spectacular place, really, like the movie epics of the time. Or, maybe, it was just that I was small then and everything looked a lot bigger."

In fact, Mrs. Nixon outdid her predecessors in Christmas decor, receptions, and entertainments, reverting to a more formal social season than the Kennedys and Johnsons had observed. Her most enduring Christmas idea was the inauguration of candlelight evening tours of the White House at Christmas, which began in 1971. On December 27 that year more than 11,000 members of the public toured the State Floor to music provided by a Marine Band string ensemble. By 1973, because of their popularity, the evening tours were extended, and by 1974, Betty Ford's first Christmas at the White House, the candlelight tours included an evening for senior citizens, another for White House staff and their families, and two more evenings for the public.

The elegance of White House events was greatly enhanced by the ever-expanding efforts to refine its historical context for interpretation. The Johnsons completed the work on the State Floor began by Mrs. Kennedy and made permanent the office of White House curator. Pat and Richard Nixon refocused the effort on furniture, acquiring priceless period pieces appropriate to their setting under the direction of Clement Conger, who also served as curator of the diplomatic reception rooms at the State Department. According to preservationist Anne Powell, the furniture and art acquired during the Nixon years represents "an interpretation that calls to mind the nineteenth century—the early White House years—and is an interpretation that remains today."

One unusual White House event initiated by the Nixons was a Christmas worship service held in the East Room. On December 20, 1970, 350 members of the administration with their children—including Alexander Shultz, Valerie Rumsfeld, Susan Haldeman, Dolly Dent, and Wendell Colson—participated in a service that featured an elaborate music program arranged by the Marine Band. On December 17, 1972, John Cardinal Krol, archbishop of Philadelphia, officiated at another Christmas service in the East Room, at which the Obernkirchen Children's Choir of Bueckeburg, Germany, accompanied by MGySgt. James Basta on the organ, sang. The following year the Rev. Dr. Billy Graham led the prayer, and the congregation joined the 36-member U.S. Army Chorus in singing hymns and carols. The idea of the Christmas services may have been prompted, in part, by the war in Vietnam.

GERALD R.
AND
ELIZABETH
WARREN
FORD
1974–77
❀

They provided an appropriately more somber and reflective context for White House Christmas parties for staff, children of diplomats, members of Congress, and the other, growing lists of events that filled the calendar from Advent to Twelfth Night.

During the 1970s Christmas themes of Americana—turkey dinner, pumpkin pie, popcorn strings, and patchwork ornaments—collided with changing public attitudes toward homemaking and homecrafts. While Betty Ford was first lady, a rapid change in public opinion took place. Society pages in the daily press began to disappear, replaced by "style" sections, covering more substantive stories about the first family. Mrs. Ford

Gerald and Betty Ford on the occasion of his swearing-in as vice president before Congress, December 6, 1973.

THE FORDS' CHRISTMAS AT VAIL

From left: Jack, Steve, Mike, Gayle, Mrs. Ford, President Ford.

Sheila Weidenfeld's journal for December 25, 1975, contains this account of the Fords' Christmas:

The Fords' tradition has become mine. For the second year in a row, I spent my early morning hours on the telephone madly scribbling the priceless give-and-take details of another First Family Christmas. Practice does not make perfect. This year it seemed to take me even longer to get my who-filled-whose-stocking-with-what lists tallied up on both the filler and fillee side (Would *Parade* magazine be interested in how I spend my Christmas?)....Lists done and fed to the reporters....

Stocking Stuffers

The President's	Filled by Gayle
Mrs. Ford's	Filled by Jack
Susan's	Filled by Mike
Jack's	Filled by Steve
Steve's	Filled by the President
Gayle's	Filled by Susan
Mike's	Filled by Mrs. Ford

began to speak out on issues affecting American women, as the traditional legion of women's page journalists, which had begun with Margaret Bayard Smith and continued for a century and a half to Betty Beale, curtailed coverage of flower arrangements and fashion but began asking hard questions on serious subjects at every opportunity.

Betty Ford's example served as a bridge arching between the more conservative and passive role played by Pat Nixon and the activist styles of Rosalynn Carter and Nancy Reagan. The Ford tenure was marked by a confusion of style and values, candor and protocol that made life in the East Wing among staff members a daily trial by fire requiring considerable wit and self-confidence. At the same time, all the old and new traditions of a White House Christmas were strictly observed—a huge ball for members of Congress, parties for staff and White House volunteers (who helped decorate for Christmas, conduct tours, and answer mail), parties for underprivileged children and the children of diplomats, annual tree-lighting and assorted receptions, state dinners, proclamations, card sending, and carolling. For the bicentennial Christmas of 1976, a press release describing the White House decorations required six pages. The tree in the Blue Room was

a 20 foot Balsam Fir ... decorated with over 2500 handmade flowers, including the state flowers of all fifty states. Materials used include silk, felt, dried cornhusks, bamboo, seeds, beads, shells, ribbon, metal, porcelain and glass. Small baskets of assorted dried flowers also are hung on the tree, which is topped with a nosegay of flowers. Tiny white lights and baby's breath complete the trimmings.

A former White House staff member commented, "Since the 1970s, each first lady tries to outdo the others. It's a never-ending spiral."

As a result of the changes in American culture at the time, the nature of the Christmas season at the White House and the role of the first lady changed. The job became one of advocacy: it became more service oriented, more political, and more sensitive to common concerns. In a large part these changes were caused by the Watergate scandal, which resulted in greater scrutiny of White House operations by the press and public. Every expense was reviewed, every word analyzed. As controversy surrounded a stream of issues relating to the "new woman," the Fords, who had been appointed rather than elected to both understudy and starring roles, were caught in the middle. Strident homemakers and religious conservatives demanded strict obedience to tradition, while a growing majority of Americans were shifting gears into a more open, egalitarian society.

When one surveys the entire social history of the White House, Betty Ford, along with Mary Lincoln, may have had the most difficult challenge in defining the role appropriate to her time. Mrs. Lincoln, in most ways, failed to recognize the special responsibilities created by war. Mrs. Ford, by contrast, seized the moment and set a new standard for candor and public service for future first ladies to follow.

Away from Washington for a winter vacation each Christmas, the Fords gathered at a condominium in Vail, Colorado, for several days of fun and photo opportunities. After the larger-than-life ambiance of the Kennedy, Johnson, and Nixon presidencies, the Fords were down to earth, stressing family ties and homemade Christmases.

CHAPTER FIFTEEN

A Dark Christmas

Like the Fords, the Carters had three older sons (Jack, Chip, and Jeff) and a daughter, Amy, who was in grade school when the family moved to Washington. The White House had not been occupied by a president who had not previously lived in Washington since Woodrow Wilson, a fellow Democrat and Georgian (Wilson, who spent his Civil War–era childhood in Augusta, Georgia, and first practiced law in Atlanta, was a contemporary of Jimmy Carter's grandfather). According to Gretchen Poston, White House social secretary for the Carter administration, "The Carters did not have a social life in Washington. In the evening, they were either attending a political event or they were at home, upstairs with their family." The three younger Carter children lived with them at the White House, and son Jack and his wife Judy, other family members, and Georgia friends were frequent visitors. Few, if any, Washingtonians penetrated the family circle.

Mrs. Ford had stepped off the society page into the news sections of the daily press, but Mrs. Carter went considerably further in creating a new role during her tenure as first lady. For the first time, the first lady had an office in the East Wing, maintained regular business hours during the week, and, with a professional staff, created a demanding schedule and a full agenda of issues. Long on substance and short on ceremony, President and Mrs. Carter relied on the White House social secretary, who traditionally works for both the president and first lady, as well as the White House permenant staff for guidance and execution of Christmas events and decorations. Decisions relating to decoration, themes, guests, and budgets were shared. "The President was as involved as anybody," recalled Poston.

For the social office the decision-making routine was exacting. Each proposed event was carefully planned and written out in a briefing book, which went up to Camp David (or wherever the Carters happened to be) each weekend. The book came back with handwritten margin notes and approvals to be implemented by the usher's, social secretary's, Park Service, and military office staffs. The usher's office included the kitchen, housekeeping, and florist staffs; the social secretary and her office invited the guests and directed the event, prepared the schedules, and were in

> JIMMY
> AND
> ROSALYNN SMITH
> CARTER
> 1977–81
> ✿

Opposite: A Victorian Christmas was the theme for White House holiday decorations in 1980.

charge of guest lists (computerized during Poston's tour of duty), calligraphy, and on occasion outside consultants. The military office provided social aides, coordinated appearances by the Marine Band and other military music groups, scheduled honor guards, and supervised other ceremonial tasks. Often, the curator's office was consulted about historical precedents or about the movement of furniture or paintings, particularly at Christmastime. When an event was planned outside the White House, the team would be substantially different, involving the press office's advance personnel, staff advance, Secret Service agents, the White House communications office, and the White House transportation office.

The budget was always tight. Twice a month the social secretary met with Hugh Carter, Jr., who was in charge of White House administration, to go over budgets and set an allotment for the next half month. With thousands of guests every month representing every conceivable constituency, there was never enough money to go around, and refreshments and other amenities were often scaled back to accommodate the full schedule of events.

Before leaving for Plains, Georgia, for the 1977 Christmas holidays, Amy placed a homemade Christmas ornament, a long green worm made from pipe cleaners, on the tree in the Blue Room. All the ornaments that year were homemade, the efforts of 1,500 retarded adults and children. One made a wedge of Swiss cheese out of styrofoam; another knitted a Star of David out of yarn. There were also strings of peanuts from Georgia and cornhusk dolls from Iowa.

In 1979, two years later, the Carter family did not make it home to Georgia for the Christmas holiday. Writing in her memoirs,

For the 1980 Christmas staff party, snow-making equipment was brought in from a ski resort for a snowman-making contest and a performance on ice by Peggy Fleming. Roasted chestnuts, hot chocolate, hot dogs, and cider were served to an outdoor assembly of more than 1,000 people.

Rosalynn remembered

instead, when the Christmas parties at the White House were over, we went up to Camp David for the remainder of the holidays. It was quiet.... We invited the senior staff at Camp David and the Filipino stewards to bring their families and join us for Christmas dinner, and all day we crossed our fingers. With negotiations for the release of the hostages [at the U.S. Embassy in Tehran, Iran] going on around the clock and the shah in Panama, I thought we just might have the most wonderful Christmas present in the world—I thought the hostages might come home. I had begun to have feelings of hope in Washington the night of the tree-lighting ceremony on the Ellipse. After Jimmy delivered a somber Christmas message to the nation, Amy pulled the switch to turn on the Christmas lights. The crowd gasped as the tree remained dark, lit only by a large star on top. "On top of the great Christmas tree is the star of hope," Jimmy's voice rang out. "We will turn on the other lights when our hostages come home, safe and free." All night and Christmas Day I was just sure we would hear good news. But the day came and went and the good news never came. Instead, two days after Christmas, there was more bad news. The Soviets had invaded Afghanistan.

The Americans in Iran had been held hostage for almost six weeks. President Carter was anxious with worry—about the hostages, the upcoming political campaign, and budget disputes—and had refrained from making political appearances. He made this entry in his diary on Christmas Day: "We made a few phone calls to my mother and others. It's relatively lonely at Camp David, just Rosalynn, Amy, and I being here. This is the first time in twenty-six years

Rosalynn Carter at diplomatic children's party, with her grandchildren, Sarah and Jason, December 15, 1980.

that I haven't been with our folks at Christmas—since the year my daddy died. Amy wanted to get up at 5:30, which we did. We had a very fine exchange of gifts."

The following year Carter and his top aides remained in the Oval Office during the holidays and into the New Year, awaiting word of the release of the hostages and counting down to their departure from the White House. The State Floor was decorated according to the theme of a Victorian Christmas, with the Blue Room tree decorated in fin de siècle finery. The National Community Christmas Tree remained dark until relatives of the hostages appealed to the president to turn the lights back on for 417 seconds on December 24—one second for each day the hostages had been in captivity. Radio stations around the country asked their listeners to step outside at 10 o'clock on Christmas Eve and turn on a light for six minutes and 57 seconds to demonstrate their support for the hostages.

CHAPTER SIXTEEN

Nancy Reagan's Perfect Christmas

Over the Labor Day weekend, 1981, Nancy Reagan's staff did not go to the beach. Instead, they were working in the West Sitting Hall of the family residence at the White House, installing and trimming a Christmas tree. The scene was staged for a photographer from *Ladies Home Journal*, which was doing a holiday article on the White House for its December edition. Because of the magazine's lead time, the pictures had to be made three months early. Celebrating the holidays at the White House requires months of planning by experts. With each successive administration, the institutional knowledge of the permanent staff grows, as does the creative and competitive impulse to top the previous year's activities and decorations.

According to James Rosebush, Mrs. Reagan's chief of staff (who also carried the title of deputy assistant to the president), planning for Christmas began by May 1, when decorating themes were discussed and a schedule was roughed out: "Since we had to plan for one to three events a day from December 1 to Christmas, the work for the holidays didn't stop."

One of the first matters to be decided

RONALD W.
AND
NANCY DAVIS
REAGAN
1981–89
❀

was the art for the annual White House Christmas card, a tradition that began at least as early as the Hoovers, but perhaps earlier. From Franklin and Eleanor Roosevelt to the Eisenhowers, the first family sent cards only to personal friends, which numbered from a few dozen to a few hundred. Eisenhower was the first to send an official card, commissioned from Hallmark, using the presidential seal. The card's basic design remained the same throughout his term, and 1,200 cards were sent each year. Kennedy sent cards to all heads of state throughout the world and expanded his list to include names beyond only personal friends, sending a total of 2,300 cards. In 1964, an election year, President Johnson sent 40,000 cards, paid for by the Democratic National Committee. No president has sent fewer cards since.

Art for the cards has varied. Only one card—the Kennedys' card of Jacqueline, Caroline, and John, Jr., with Macaroni in the snow on the South Lawn—has used a photograph. The Johnsons, after once using the presidential seal, commissioned several watercolor renderings of various White House interiors by Ohio artist Robert Laes-

Opposite: President Reagan surveys Christmas decorations in the East Room, 1981.

"After the Kennedy Center Honors in early December, we shut the White House for two days to decorate," explained James Rosebush, who served as Nancy Reagan's chief of staff. Florists from around the country came in to help, along with White House staff florists, electricians, carpenters, housekeepers, and secretaries.

sig. Many of the cards in the Nixon, Ford, and Carter years used reproductions of prints and paintings from the White House collection. The Reagans commissioned several contemporary American artists to design cards around White House views. Jamie Wyeth designed two cards (a reproduction of a work by his grandfather, N.C. Wyeth, was used during the Nixon years), Thomas William Jones provided art for four cards, and James Steinmeyer and Mark Hampton, an interior designer involved in the White House and Blair House restoration projects, have each designed a card. By 1983 the Reagan card list had grown to include 75,000 names; the Republican National Committee paid for the printing and mailing of the cards. The Bushes also used a Hampton watercolor for their 1990 card, which depicted the Oval Office with a Christmas tree; 145,000 cards were mailed.

Christmas cards reach the widest group of people who are in the White House orbit, while the work of the chefs in the

White House kitchen is known to only a select few—those invited to the White House for dinner. The concoctions of Roland Mesnier, the Reagan's pastry chef, were a far cry from the plum puddings and fruit cakes that Henrietta Nesbitt prepared for Franklin and Eleanor Roosevelt. According to Mesnier, baking for the Reagan's first White House Christmas, "dessert is very, very important. To them, it is the main thing.… I'm really amazed. They may cut something else out, but not dessert." For Christmas dinner that year the stuffed turkey and marshmallow sweet potatoes were topped off with a yule log made of graduated layers of meringue and kirsch-flavored pistachio ice cream and covered with chocolate. The decorations—holly leaves, Santas, and fruits—were made of marzipan.

For confections to be used for display, the first lady turned to Hans Raffert, assistant executive chef, to build a gingerbread house for the State Dining Room, his calling since 1969, when he built his first one for the Nixons. Giving it a Reagan touch, the 1981 model featured a jelly bean chimney. That year he also illuminated the windows, which glowed red, blue, and green, representing the three parlors on the State Floor. Raffert's creation was no small feat. This gingerbread house was 3 feet tall, 2 feet wide, and 16 inches deep and weighed 45 pounds. The figures of Hansel, Gretel, a witch, and a snowman, made of marzipan, were placed in the front yard. The house was decorated with 6 pounds of German cookies, 1 pound of candy canes, 2 pounds of hard candies, 15 pounds of royal icing, 20 pounds of gingerbread dough, and one pound of confectioners sugar to imitate fallen snow.

Like other first ladies of the recent past, Mrs. Reagan appeared at various photo opportunities to help usher in the holidays. Welcoming the season in a parade of red dresses and big smiles, Mrs. Reagan posed while awaiting the arrival of the White House Christmas tree, while on a guided tour with Mr. T, Dom DeLuise, and Ed McMahon, while hanging ornaments on the tree, and while standing with family members by the tree in the family residence. At each click of the shutter, another phase of the season was revealed, providing Americans through television, newspapers, and magazines a seamless ballet of ebullient fun and good living under the mistletoe.

Always trailing behind the ubiquitous photographers and film crews were the reporters—relentless, persistent, and seemingly immune to the spirit of Christmas. The press corps refused to sit still for prepackaged stories. In December 1986 as she walked members of the press through the elaborately decorated rooms on the State Floor, Mrs. Reagan had to deny that she and the president were having a fight over Chief of Staff Donald Regan. "We disagree sometimes," said Mrs. Reagan. "Everybody does." Then a reporter reminded the first lady that the president had likened the press to "circling sharks" in its coverage of the Iran-Contra affair. "I'll bet you've said things you wouldn't want repeated," she replied. On and on it went, contin-

uing the next evening at a Christmas party for the press. Reagan's allusion, originally from a *Time* article by Hugh Sidey, was repeated in the *Washington Post*'s coverage: "'There is a bitter bile in my throat these days. I've never seen the sharks circling like they now are with blood in the water.... The whole thing boils down to a great irresponsibility on the part of the press." NBC correspondent Chris Wallace admitted, "I give the president and Mrs. Reagan high marks for showing up and standing there for an hour, shaking hands with some people that they probably don't like too much right now."

Arms and hostages, irregular campaign finances and rogue staff members, Oliver North and Swiss bank accounts—all were fodder for the ever-vigilant press even at Christmastime. Through the Reagan years the image of the media and press is best portrayed by television reporter Sam Donaldson, shouting across the lawn over the deafening whip of the helicopter blades, telling rude and bad jokes to no one in particular in a loud falsetto. If Christmas was off limits, no one told the men and women of the media. Even when they tried to be nice, they failed. ABC correspondent Kenneth Walker was quoted in the *Post* as saying, regarding the Iran-Contra scandal, "I mentioned to the president that I hoped the present difficulties would not prevent him from having a merry Christmas."

Mrs. Reagan and Dom DeLuise at the 1987 unveiling of the White House Christmas decorations.

CHAPTER SEVENTEEN

At Home with the Bush Family

During the 1990 Christmas season, the American people were riveted to their television screens, watching the disintegration of the Iron Curtain. President Bush declared that

throughout Central and Eastern Europe, Christmas songs will trumpet from radios again this year... In Poland, people can sing a verse to an ancient hymn that has been silent since 1946.... In Berlin, there are no walls to stop carollers.... For thousands of Jews exiting the Soviet Union this year, Chanukah will have a special meaning.... We may speak different languages and attend different places of worship, but our hope and our faith in the universal dream of peace and freedom is a common bond that unites us all.

In his Christmas message President Bush, like most modern U.S. presidents, entwined the holiday with the American idea of freedom, expressing in words the television images of jubilant people in city squares—Prague, Budapest, Warsaw, and Sofia—their smiling faces glowing in the light of thousands of flickering candles. Christmas messages by presidents, often delivered at the lighting of the National Community Christmas Tree, go back a hundred years to 1891, when Benjamin Harrison told a New York jour-

---

> GEORGE H. W.
> AND
> BARBARA PIERCE
> BUSH
> 1989–
> ✤

---

nalist that "Christmas ... should be an occasion of general rejoicing throughout the land, from the humblest citizen to the highest official...." Other Christmas comment emanated from Washington over the years, and in 1927 Calvin Coolidge inaugurated the annual Christmas message from the White House, a tradition that endures. "It is not easy to say 'Merry Christmas' to you, my fellow Americans, in this time of destructive war, " said Franklin Roosevelt on his last Christmas Eve. "Nor can I say 'Merry Christmas' lightly tonight to our armed forces at their battle stations all over the world—and to our allies who fight by their side." For Truman, Christmas was a occasion to remind Americans of the religious significance of the holiday, while Eisenhower framed his messages to include various subjects, including traffic safety, poverty, and freedom, and to address specific groups—the Boy Scouts, the Girl Scouts, the U.S. armed forces, and the people of Eastern Europe.

Kennedy emphasized the celebration of Christmas across cultures, including Moslems, Hindus, and Buddhists as well as Christians, calling it "a universal holiday of

Opposite: Barbara Bush, with granddaughter Marshall Bush and a U.S. Park Service official, places a star atop the 1989 National Community Christmas Tree on the Ellipse.

On Christmas Eve, 1989, 23
members of the Bush family
(including "First Dog" Millie)
gather at Camp David.

all men." War and peace, recession and prosperity, freedom and oppression, and love and friendship have been the texts of each Christmas keynote through the years, indicating a pause from partisanship and summoning hope with a call for merriment and good cheer.

George Bush, who took office on the bicentennial of the presidency, shared with the first president, George Washington, the date of his wedding anniversary, January 6. In fact, Bush had planned to marry Barbara Pierce a week before Christmas, but his plane was shot down over the Pacific, delaying the festivities until Twelfth Night.

The series of events for Barbara and George Bush's first White House Christmas began with a press preview on December 11 and did not stop until Christmas. These events included a congressional Christmas ball, a reception for the children of diplomats, various staff parties, and a series of East Room Christmas receptions over seven evenings that accommodated thousands of

guests, an entertaining plan that was repeated the following year.

Upstairs, the Yellow Oval Room was cluttered with books and toys, evidence of a gaggle of grandchildren, infants to preteens, numbering a baker's dozen and given free reign. On the Sunday before Christmas a brunch was organized in the West Hall, as family members and friends arrived from Texas, Virginia, Florida, and Colorado.

The following week members of the public arrived in the evening through the East Foyer, bedecked with a Christmas fantasy of snowy evergreens, and passed red poinsettia "trees" and tall teakwood candlestands burning red wax candles. Going up the stair and emerging into the East Room, visitors found the Engelhard crèche, flanked by four 10-foot-tall blue spruce trees decorated with red velvet and gold ribbon garlands, Florentine angels, gold balls, and miniature musical instruments. On each of the four mantels were matching wreaths. Two dozen trees, dusted with artificial snow and decorated with miniature white lights and garlands of greens with red ribbons lined the Grand Foyer, where the brass choir of the Marine Band with polished shoes and Christmas-red jackets played seasonal music. In the Blue Room stood a mighty 18½-foot-tall Fraser fir, grown by Mike and Bruce Lacey of Newland, North Carolina, named the 1990 national grand champion growers by the National Christmas Tree Association. The theme of the tree decorations was *The Nutcracker*, Tchaikovsky's ballet, and featured 50 pairs of ballet slippers, 40 porcelain dancers, 100 velvet balls, silk flowers (one of each state flower), lace and ribbons, assorted hand-blown glass ornaments from the White House collection, and on a table the young prince's castle in the Land of Sweets. Next door, in the State Dining Room, chef Raffert presented his 21st gingerbread house.

As visitors paused along the way, they were serenaded by carollers from the Soul Children of Chicago or one of 50 other groups who performed for public tours during the 1990 Christmas season. Outside, a queue wound around the edge of the South Lawn. Visitors could look up to the Truman Balcony, just inside the center window, and see where George and Barbara Bush had placed their personal tree. Across the street the National Community Christmas Tree and the Pageant of Peace provided additional wonders for children and their parents.

The Bushes were at Camp David, but the mansion remained illuminated during the evening for sightseers. The traffic passed along Pennsylvania Avenue, slowing to a

crawl as drivers and their passengers peered into the night, across the lawn and through the White House windows. Wreaths were hung in each of the 16 windows. Beneath the North Portico hung a lantern, a beacon for guests, draped with greenery and trimmed with red bows, first decorated in this manner by Theodore and Edith Roosevelt to welcome their Christmas guests. The view is the same in 1992 as in 1902.

In 1913 Franklin D. Roosevelt, then assistant secretary of the navy, called on the legendary Henry Adams, who lived in a house facing Lafayette Park. Roosevelt, praising his boss, President Wilson, drew a laugh from Adams, who was John Quincy's grandson and the great-grandson of the first occupant of the President's House. "Young man," he said, pointing to the White House, "it does not make the slightest difference who lives in that house, history goes on with or without the president."

For a decade film and television producer George Stevens, Jr., has presented a gala television special, "A Celebration of Christmas in Washington," from the Pension Building (now the National Building Museum) for the benefit of Children's Hospital National Medical Center. In the 1990 NBC broadcast John Denver (right) hosted an evening of entertainment that featured Aretha Franklin (left). Mrs. Bush (center) and three of her grandchildren, Ellie LeBlond (left), Marshall Bush (center), and Sam LeBlond (right), join the performers on stage for "Hark! The Herald Angels Sing."

Afterword: Symbols of an American Christmas

The White House serves primarily as the residence of the first family, secondarily as the executive offices of the president, a place where state and other ceremonial functions take place, and also as a museum, receiving 1.5 million visitors a year. The distinctions among these functions often overlap, creating ambiguities and requiring tough decisions for the permanent White House staff. "I think everything we do in this house is a compromise," says Rex Scouten, White House curator. He imagines someday "the family living elsewhere and the house being used for official entertaining and as a museum.... They really don't have any privacy. They have their bedroom and maybe one other room that is really theirs...."

When I began to conduct research for *A White House Christmas*, it was not at all clear to me which function of the Executive Mansion—home, office, reception hall, or museum—prevailed in the celebration of Christmas. Because it was a government building, I wondered if the usual observances of Christmas celebrations in American life were in any way proscribed by the establishment clause of the first amendment to the Constitution.

In fact, the path of American history that leads to religious freedom is littered with good intentions—some supported, others stricken—by the courts. In its subtlety and uniqueness, the establishment clause has caused considerable confusion over the years.

The Constitution says, "Congress shall make no law respecting the establishment of religion, or prohibiting the free exercise thereof"—the purpose of which, Thomas Jefferson explained in 1802, was to build "a wall of separation between Church and State." The doorways through this wall have been sufficient for church and state to live comfortably with each other most of the time for two centuries. The government provides tax exemptions for religious property and has permitted Sunday closing laws; it provides for conscientious objection and alternative service for people who have religious scruples against participating in combat or military service. The courts have permitted students certain absences from school for religious observances and have sanctioned chaplains and prayers in Congress and other government bodies.

The pivotal case relating to Christmas, *Lynch v. Donnelly* (465 U.S. 668), was decided in 1984 in a split decision by the U.S. Supreme Court, which found that officials in Pawtucket, Rhode Island, could place a Nativity scene on public property as

Opposite: White House Grand Staircase decorated for Christmas, 1972.

part of an official Christmas observance without violating the principle of separation of church and state. Chief Justice Warren Burger, writing for the majority, found that "the City has a secular purpose for including the crèche, that the City has not impermissibly advanced religion, and that including the crèche does not create excessive entanglement between religion and government." In a separate concurring opinion, Associate Justice Sandra Day O'Connor found that "what is crucial is that a government practice not have the effect of communicating a message of government endorsement or disapproval of religion." Justice William Brennan wrote the dissent, joined by Thurgood Marshall, Harry Blackmun, and John Paul Stevens, which was concerned with the integrity of religion and the trivializing of its symbols. He found that the crèche was not a mere historical representation but "is instead best understood as a mystical recreation of an event that lies at the heart of the Christian faith."

Christian and Jewish leaders are divided on the subject. The Reverend Dean Kelly of the National Council of Churches remarked that "to take the most sacred symbols of one religious group and desacralize them as just one in a row of secular folk symbols like Santa Claus and Rudolph the Red-Nosed Reindeer is a great loss to the religious groups that view those symbols as sacred," while Monsignor Daniel Hoyle of the U. S. Catholic Conference and Jerry Falwell of the Moral Majority concurred with the Pawtucket decision. Jewish leaders also disagree among themselves. Members of the arch-conservative Lubavitch movement have generally supported the use of religious symbols in public places in a effort to place the Chanukah menorah in proximity to a crèche or Christmas tree. The rest of the Jewish community, led by the American Jewish Congress, generally has opposed all religious displays on public property.

When Calvin Coolidge first inaugurated the National Community Christmas Tree in 1923, religious issues were tempered by commercial considerations. The Potomac Electric and Power Company sought to encourage the use of electric lights on trees, and the insurance industry was behind the event because of the high incidence of fires caused by Christmas trees lighted with candles.

The simple Christmas message of George and Barbara Bush sums up the sentiments of all recent presidents of the United States, who have sought to maintain a balance between their appeal for peace in the world and an expression of good tidings to the American people: "The President and Mrs. Bush extend their warmest wishes for a merry Christmas and a new year that will bring harmony to our world and happiness to you and those you love."

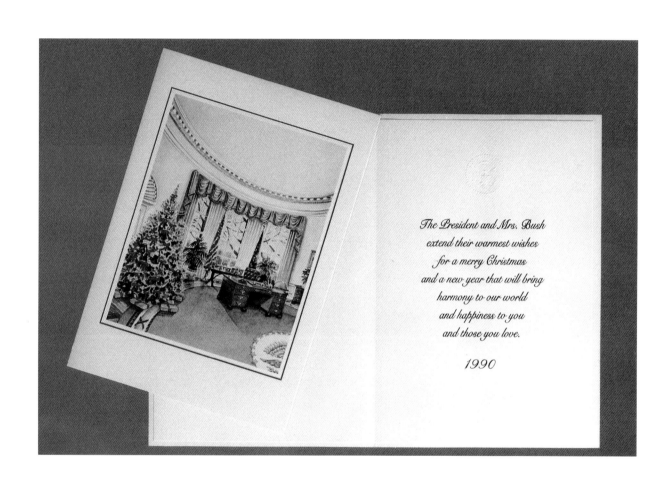

The President and Mrs. Bush
extend their warmest wishes
for a merry Christmas
and a new year that will bring
harmony to our world
and happiness to you
and those you love.

1990

"President's Levee—Portico of
the White House," *Illustrated
News*, November 19, 1853.

Bibliographical Notes

Chapter 1: George and Martha's Twelfth Night

For detailed accounts of George Washington's whereabouts during the Christmas and New Year's season of various years and for quotations from his letters, see Elizabeth B. Johnston, *George Washington Day by Day* (New York: Cycle Publishing Co., 1895); Mary V. Thompson's study guide "Information Drawn from George Washington's Diaries and Writings Relative to the Christmas Season with Family and Friends" (Mount Vernon, Va.: Mount Vernon Ladies' Association of the Union, 1990); see also Harnett T. Kane, *The Southern Christmas Book* (New York: David McKay, 1958); Benjamin James and Fritzie James, *Christmas with George Washington 1776–1799* (Philadelphia: Franklin Printing Co., 1954); Olive Bailey, *Christmas with the Washingtons* (Richmond, Va.: Dietz Press, 1948); and Karal Ann Marling, *George Washington Slept Here* (Cambridge, Mass.: Harvard University Press, 1988).

For a discussion of Christmas in the American colonies and England during the Restoration, see Ruth Cole Kainen, *America's Christmas Heritage* (New York: Funk and Wagnalls, 1969); Miles Hadfield and John Hadfield, *The Twelve Days of Christmas* (Boston: Little, Brown and Co., 1961); and R. J. Mitchell and M. D. R. Leys, *A History of London Life* (London:

Longsmans, Green and Co., 1958).

An authoritative genealogical reference work for families of presidents of the United States is Hugh Montgomery-Massingberd, ed., *Burke's Presidential Families of the United States of America*, 2d ed. (London: Burke's Peerage, 1981). See also Sandra L. Quinn and Sanford Kanter, *America's Royalty* (Westport, Conn.: Greenwood Press, 1983); J. J. Perling, *Presidents' Sons* (New York: Odyssey Press, 1947); Stephen Hess, *America's Political Dynasties* (Garden City, N.Y.: Doubleday and Co., 1966); and Edward Pessen, *Log Cabin Myth* (New Haven, Conn.: Yale University Press, 1984).

Chapter 2: A Home for the Holidays

The best sources for accounts of social life during the early years of the White House are Esther Singleton, *Story of the White House* (London: Hodder and Stoughton, 1908); Margaret Bayard Smith, *The First Forty Years of Washington Society* (New York: Frederick Ungar Publishing Co., 1965); and William Seale, *The President's House* (Washington, D. C.: White House Historical Association, 1986).

For collections of presidents' and first ladies' letters, see Edwin Morris Betts and James Adam Bear, Jr., *The Family Letters of Thomas Jefferson* (Columbia: University of Missouri Press, 1966);

Adrienne Koch and William Peden, eds., *Life and Selected Writings of Thomas Jefferson* (New York: Random House, 1944); Allen C. Clark, *Life and Letters of Dolley Madison* (Washington, D.C.: Press of W. F. Roberts Co., 1914); and Allan Nevins, ed., *The Diary of John Quincy Adams* (New York: Frederick Ungar Publishing Co., 1951); see also Betty Boyd Caroli's excellent social history *First Ladies* (New York: Oxford University Press, 1987).

There is no Washington Irving biography in print. Irving's *The Sketch Book of Geoffrey Crayon, Gent.* (New York: Dodd, Mead and Co., 1954) was consulted; to follow Irving's and other American diplomats peregrinations through England, see Brian N. Morton, *Americans in London* (New York: William Morrow and Co., 1986).

Material on St. John's Church was found in St. John's Church archives: Alexander B. Hagner, *History and Reminiscences of St. John's Church, 1816–1905* (Washington, D. C.: St. John's Church, 1906). For an 1817 description of Elizabeth Monroe, see Peter Hay, *All the President's Ladies* (New York: Viking, 1988), 53. Early accounts of Christmas in Alexandria, Virginia were assembled for Lloyd House, Library of Virginia History and Genealogy, by James Munson, "Signs of the Times," *The Fireside Sentinel* (January 10, 1987), 82–85; see also John Francis, "Christmas Times," *Alexandria Gazette*, December 21, 1840.

Chapter 3: A People's Christmas

The celebration of Christmas in America in the early 19th century is well documented in Katherine Lambert Richards, *How Christmas Came to the Sunday-Schools* (New York: Dodd, Mead and Co., 1934); see also James H. Barnett, *American Christmas: A Study in National Culture* (New York: Macmillan, 1954). For Christmas accounts from the mid-19th century, particularly in New York, see Phillip V. Snyder, *December 25th, The Joys of Christmas Past* (New York: Dodd, Mead and Co., 1985).

For accounts of the first Christmas trees, see Phillip V. Snyder, *The Christmas Tree Book* (New York: Viking Press, 1976); and Nada Gray, *Holidays: Victorian Women Celebrate in Pennsylvania* (University Park: Pennsylvania State University Press, 1983).

Mary Randolph's *The Virginia Housewife* (1824), edited by Karen Hess (Columbia: University of South Carolina Press, 1984) is a cookbook of early American recipes that has been a popular standard for generations; this edition includes an excellent essay by Hess on early 19th-century cookery. See also Kathryn Grover, ed., *Dining in America 1850-1900* (Amherst: University of Massachusetts Press, 1987); Barbara G. Carson, *Ambitious Appetite* (Washington, D. C.: American Institute of Architects Press, 1990); and Linda Wolfe, *The Literary Gourmet* (New York: Simon and Schuster, 1985).

For an account of Christmases in the Andrew Jackson White House, see Mary Emily Donelson Wilcox, *Christmas Under Three Flags* (Washington, D.C.: The Neale Publishing Co., 1900).

Chapter 4: An Antebellum Christmas in Washington

There are several fascinating travellers' accounts of Washington, D.C., before the Civil War. From the 1830s, see Francis J. Grund's 1839 journal, *Aristocracy in America* (New York: Harper and Brothers, Publishers, 1959); Frances M. Trollope, *Domestic Manners of the Americans* (New York: Howard Wilford Bell, 1904); Alexis de Tocqueville, *Democracy in America* (New York: Penguin Books, 1984); Harriet Martineau, *Society in America* (Gloucester, Mass: Peter Smith, 1962). See also Eyre Crowe, *With Thackeray in America* (New York: Charles Scribner's Sons, 1893), 120; Edgar Johnson, *Charles Dickens: His Tragedy and Triumph* (New York: Simon and Schuster, 1952); and Norman MacKenzie and Jeanne MacKenzie, *Dickens, A Life* (New York: Oxford University Press, 1979). For an account of the first meeting between Dickens and Irving, see Una Pope-Hennessy, *Charles Dickens* (London: The Reprint Society, 1945), 172; for comment on Dickens from Thackeray, see William M. Thackeray, "Christmas Carol," *Fraser's Magazine,* February, 1844, 48; see also Russell Lynes, *The Domesticated Americans* (New York: Harper and Row, Publishers, 1963), 148-49, including his quotation from Mark Twain's *The Gilded Age.*

For quotations from John Tyler, see Robert Seager II, *And Tyler Too* (New York: McGraw-Hill, 1963).

Documentation relating to Christmas and the Presbyterian church is found in *Digest of Acts and Proceedings of the General Assembly of the Presbyterian Church in the United States, 1861–1944* (Richmond, Va.: Presbyterian Committee of Publications, 1945). For Polk's observance of the Sabbath, see Allan Nevins, ed., *Polk: The Diary of a President 1845–1849* (London: Longsmans, Green and Co., 1952), 179; for a description of slavery in the District of Columbia, see 359. For other discussions of slavery, see Edmund Fuller and David E. Green, *God in the White House* (New York: Crown Publishers, 1968), 85; and Harriet Martineau, *Society in America*, 12.

A visit to the White House was recorded by Joanna Lucinda Rucker [Mrs. Polk's niece], unpublished letter dated January 7, 1846, to Elizabeth C. Price, Murfreesboro, Tennessee (White House Curator's Office).

Chapter 5: A Blue and Gray Christmas

Jackson's quote about Buchanan is from Paul F. Boller, Jr., *Presidential Anecdotes* (New York: Oxford University Press, 1981), 119. The story of Harriet Lane at Buckingham Palace was found in Bess Furman, *White House Profile* (Indianapolis: Bobbs-Merrill Co., 1951), 163. For Buchanan's liquor order, see Philip S. Klein, *President James Buchanan* (Philadelphia: J. B. Lippincott and Co., 1962), 6. For the account of Schell and Lane, see Peter Hay, *All the President's Ladies* (New York: Viking, 1988), 7-8; for an explanation of the social order, January 1, 1858, William Seale, *The President's House* (Washington, D. C.: White House Historical Association, 1986), 349.

The Christmas, 1860, diary entry was quoted from Everette B. Long, ed., *The Civil War Day by Day* (Garden City, N.Y.: Doubleday and Co, 1971), 15. Lincoln's favorite story about himself comes from Paul F. Boller, Jr., *Presidential Anecdotes*, 157. For the best stories about Tad Lincoln, see Ruth Painter Randall, *Lincoln's Sons* (Boston: Little, Brown and Co., 1955);

Christmas, 1863, 140; East Room, 125; Stuntz Toy Store,140; Aunt Emilie's visit, 130; other Tad Lincoln stories, 87–88, 143. For the conversation with Mary Lincoln regarding state dinners, see Elizabeth Keckley's 1868 diary, *Behind the Scenes: Thirty Years a Slave and Four Years in the White House,* edited by William L. Katz (New York: Arno Press, 1968), 96.

The story of Arlington House and General Lee came from Judy Frank, "Tidings from Gen. Robert E. Lee: His Son Wasn't Home for Holidays," *Washington Times,* December 15, 1988, C-1; for the account of the Emancipation Proclamation, see William Seale, *The President's House* (Washington, D.C.: White House Historical Association, 1986), 406.

See also Carl Sandburg, *Abraham Lincoln, The Prairie Years and The War Years* (New York: Harcourt Brace Jovanovich, 1926); and Jean H. Baker, *Mary Todd Lincoln, A Biography* (New York: W. W. Norton and Co., 1987).

Chapter 6: Deck the Halls

For the account of the Lincolns and the Johnsons, see W. H. Crook, *Memories of the White House* (Boston: Little, Brown and Co., 1911), 78. The Ben Perley Poore quote is from Ona G. Jeffries, *In and Out of the White House* (New York: Wilfred Funk, 1961), 200. King Kalakaua's visit was reported in "Our Royal Visitor," *The Evening Star,* December 14, 1874, 1; and "Society, Etc.," *The Evening Star,* December 23, 1874, 1. Grant's taste in music was recorded in Elise Kirk, *Music at the White House* (Urbana: University of Illinois Press, 1986), 103. For the remark regarding Tilden, see Robert Radcrift, "White House Memories Span 175 Christmases," *National Geographic Society News Feature,* December 2, 1975, 1. One of the many

accounts of the Hayeses' anniversary reception is "Our Washington Letter," *Albany Evening Journal,* January 3, 1878, 1. A record of Hayes's diary entry, December 25, 1880, was found in *Diary and Letters of Rutherford Birchard Hayes,* vol. 3 (Columbus: Ohio State Archæological and Historical Society, 1924), 631–32. A notice of the F Street dance was found in "Society," *The Evening Star,* December 24, 1887, 1. For the report of the New Year's reception, 1882, see Emily E. Briggs, *The Olivia Letters* (New York: The Neale Publishing Co., 1906), 430–31. See also Emily Apt Geer, *First Lady, The Life of Lucy Webb Hayes* (Kent, Ohio: Kent State University Press, 1984).

Chapter 7: O Tannenbaum

Sen. Foraker's comment is found in Carl S. Anthony, *First Ladies* (New York: William Morrow and Co., 1990), 268. The account of President Arthur and Sousa is found in Elise Kirk, *Music at the White House* (Urbana: University of Illinois Press, 1986), 136. Cecil Spring Rice is quoted by Henry F. Pringle, *Life and Times of William Howard Taft* (Hamden, Conn.: Archon Books, 1964), 112–13. The recognition of Christmas is discussed in James H. Barnett, *American Christmas: A Study in National Culture* (New York: Macmillan, 1954), 20–21.

The first White House Christmas tree is described by W. H. Crook, *Memories of the White House* (Boston: Little, Brown and Co., 1911), 205–6. For the turkey recipe, see Caroline L. (Mrs. Benjamin) Harrison, *Statesmen's Dishes and How to Cook Them* (Washington, D. C.: The National Tribune Publishing Co., 1890). For the remark "wine flowed like water," see Irwin H. Hoover, *Forty-Two Years in the White House* (Boston: Houghton Mifflin Co.,

1934), 288. Mary Harrison McKee's letter was published as "Christmas Letter to Robert McKee–1889," *The Harrison Home Statesman,* December, 1976, 1–2.

No legislative history on federal holiday pay policies before 1875 exists. Information was pieced together from a variety of legislative references, with assistance provided by the library staff of the Office of Personnel Management. For an introduction to the subject, see Ismar Baruch, "Federal Holiday Pay Policies," *Personnel Administration* 8, 1 (1945), 15–18.

Chapter 8: A Great Big Lovable Teddy Bear

For accounts of Christmas at Sagamore Hill, see Carolyn J. Mazzeo, "The Roosevelt Family Christmas 1898–1918," (Washington, D.C.: U.S. Park Service, 1978). The origins of the teddy bear come from Peggy Bialosky and Alan Bialosky, *The Teddy Bear Catalog* (New York: Workman Publishing Co., 1980), 12–16. Roosevelt's letter to James Garfield was found in Joseph B. Bishop, ed., *Theodore Roosevelt's Letters to His Children* (New York: Charles Scribner's Sons, 1919). For the account of Roosevelt in Rome, see Corinne Roosevelt Robinson, *My Brother, Theodore Roosevelt* (New York: Charles Scribner's Sons, 1921), 48–49, For other childhood stories, see Theodore Roosevelt, *Theodore Roosevelt: An Autobiography* (New York: Macmillan and Co., 1913), 8; Robinson, 48; and Theodore Roosevelt III, *All in the Family* (New York: G. P. Putnam's Sons, 1929), 138.

The description of the cabinet dinner, 1902, was prepared by the officer in charge of public buildings and found in "Social Functions," December 18 journal entry, 1902–16, Record Group 42, National Archives and Records

Administration, Washington, D.C. Stories about and quotations from Alice Longworth came from Alice Longworth, *Crowded Hours* (New York: Charles Scribner's Sons, 1933), 47, 161; and from Michael Teague, *Mrs. L: Conversations with Alice Roosevelt Longworth* (Garden City, N. Y.: Doubleday and Co., 1981), 114. For accounts of Archibald and Quentin, see Frances Cavanah, *They Lived in the White House* (Philadelphia: Macrae Smith Co., 1959), 120.

Chapter 9: Christmas and the American Spirit

Taft's shopping excursions are described in Archibald W. Butt, *The Letters of Archie Butt* (Garden City, N. Y.: Doubleday, Page and Co., 1924), 240–43. For Butt's eggnog recipe, see Archibald W. Butt, *Taft and Roosevelt*, vol. 1 (Garden City, N.Y.: Doubleday, Doran and Co., 1930), 248; see also Edwin C. Bearss, *Historic Data—Home: William Howard Taft National Historic Site* (Washington, D.C.: National Park Service, U.S. Department of Interior, 1972).

For an account of the Wilson honeymoon, see Thomas Shachtman, *Edith and Woodrow: A Presidential Romance* (New York: G. P. Putnam's Sons, 1981), 124. For the story of the Wilsons' trip to Europe at the end of World War I, see Edith Bolling Wilson, *My Memoir* (Indianapolis: Bobbs-Merrill Co., 1938), 189–90.

The description of Christmas, 1922, came from Evalyn Walsh McLean, *Father Struck It Rich* (New York: Arno Press, 1975), 256–57. The Eugene Debs account came from Alice Terry White, *Eugene Debs* (New York: Lawrence Hill and Co., 1974), 129. Also consulted was Francis Russell, *The Shadow of Blooming Grove:*

Warren G. Harding in His Times (New York: McGraw Hill, 1968).

For the Coolidges' Christmases, see Isabel Ross, *Grace Coolidge and Her Era* (New York: Dodd, Mead and Co., 1962), 111, 170. For the correspondence relating to the first community Christmas tree, see Lucretia Hardy's letters, November 30, 1923, and December 4, 1923, Record Group 120, National Archives and Records Administration, Washington, D.C. Other Christmas-related information can be found in William Allen White, *A Puritan in Babylon* (New York: The MacMillan Co., 1938).

Franklin Roosevelt's comment about Hoover is from Hugh Montgomery-Massingberd, ed., *Burke's Presidential Families of the United States of America*, 2d ed. (London: Burke's Peerage, 1981), 469. See also Arthur M. Schlesinger, Jr. *Crisis of the Old Order* (Boston: Houghton Mifflin, 1957). The accounts relating to New Year's receptions came from Herbert Clark Hoover, *The Memoirs of Herbert Hoover* (New York: The MacMillan Co., 1952), 323, 326. The Bess Furman story is from Betty Caroli's *First Ladies* (New York: Oxford University Press, 1987), 183.

Chapter 10: Eleanor's Year-Round Christmases

The quotation "Eleanor was my brother Ted's favorite" is from Corinne Roosevelt Robinson, *My Brother, Theodore Roosevelt* (New York: Charles Scribner's Sons, 1921), 73. "Eleanor Roosevelt's Christmas Gift Books," 1922–34, 1935–62, were found in the Anna Eleanor Roosevelt Papers, Franklin D. Roosevelt Library, Hyde Park, New York. For correspondence relating to the Christmas tree farm, see Grace

Tully memorandum to Mr. Plog concerning Christmas tree to Churchill, Presidential Social Files, Franklin D. Roosevelt Papers, Franklin D. Roosevelt Library, Hyde Park, N.Y. For Nelson C. Brown letter concerning Christmas trees and account of the 1943 Christmas tree, see folder, Presidential Social Files, Franklin D. Roosevelt Papers, Franklin D. Roosevelt Library, Hyde Park, N.Y.

For descriptions of White House Christmases, see Anna Eleanor Roosevelt, *Eleanor Roosevelt's Christmas Book* (New York: Dodd, Mead and Co., 1963), 6–9. The Ruby A. Black letter to the White House, 1936, was found in the Anna Eleanor Roosevelt Papers, Franklin D. Roosevelt Library, Hyde Park, New York. Descriptions of foods and menus came from Henrietta Nesbitt, *White House Diary* (Garden City, N.Y.: Doubleday and Co., 1949), 68–69, 95–96. For Churchill's visit to the White House in 1941, see Kay Halle, ed., *Winston Churchill on America and Britain* (New York: Walker and Co., 1970), xxv, 90; and Edith B. Helm, *The Captains and the Kings* (New York: G. P. Putnam's Sons, 1954). Parallels in the life of career of Theodore Roosevelt and Franklin Roosevelt are also discussed at length in Arthur Schlesinger, Jr. *Crisis of the Old Order*, 317-55.

Chapter 11: A Month of Christmases

For the description of home life at the White House, see Anna Eleanor Roosevelt, *Eleanor Roosevelt's Christmas Book* (New York: Dodd, Mead and Co., 1963), 6. The account of Christmas, 1945, came from Margaret Truman, *Bess W. Truman* (New York: Macmillan Publishing Co., 1986), 281. Also of interest are Margaret Truman, *White House Pets* (New York: David

McKay Co., 1969), and Jhan Robbins, *Bess and Harry* (New York: G. P. Putnam's Sons, 1980).

Desciptions of White House receptions are found in William Seale, *The President's House* (Washington, D.C.: White House Historical Association, 1986), 1,022. For the most complete description of the White House reconstruction, see Seale, 1,037; and Anne Elizabeth Powell, "President's House," *Historic Preservation,* May-June, 1991, 25–26.

Eisenhower guest lists came from Mary Van Rensselaer Thayer, *Jacqueline Kennedy: The White House Years* (Boston: Little, Brown and Co., 1971), 183. The quotation "squealing with delight,"came from "Past Christmases at the White House," White House Social Office memorandum, 1970, White House Curator's Office, Washington, D.C. Quotations from Dwight David Eisenhower II are from a telephone interview with author, January 23, 1991. The "Text of Eisenhower Yule Message" is from the *New York Times*, December 24, 1960, 13.

Chapter 12: Christmas at Camelot

For Mrs. Eisenhower's correspondence, see Mamie Eisenhower Autograph file, 1955, Daughters of the American Revolution Archives, Washington, D. C. The quotation beginning "gaiety, informality and culture" is from Mary Van Rensselaer Thayer, *Jacqueline Kennedy: The White House Years* (Boston: Little, Brown and Co., 1971), 181. The Edward R. Carr letter regarding the Pagaent of Peace to Mr. John McNally, November 5, 1962, and the Pagaent of Peace invitation, 1962, were found at the John F. Kennedy Library, Boston, Massachusetts.

13. The Gilded Cage

For the account of Christmas, 1965, see Elizabeth Carpenter, White House press release, December 20, 1965, Lyndon Baines Johnson Library, Austin, Texas. For the description of Prime Minister Wilson's visit, see Connie Dunaway, memorandum for Mrs. Bess Abel, December 14, 1965, Lyndon Baines Johnson Library, Austin, Texas, and Angier Biddle Duke, "Visit to the United States of America of the Right Honorable Harold Wilson, O. B. E., M. P., Prime Minister of the United Kingdom. Administrative Arrangements for the Arrival at the White House Monday, December 7, 1964, 11:15 a.m.," memorandum, 1964, Lyndon Baines Johnson Library, Austin, Texas.

The "Briefing for the Wedding" came from a memorandum, 1967, Lyndon Baines Johnson Library, Austin, Texas. The story of the crèche came from Jane Engelhard, letter to Mrs. Lyndon Johnson, March 16, 1967; Jane Engelhard, letter to Bess Abell, June 10, 1967; and Jane Engelhard, "Christmas Cribs for the White House," (report), April 14, 1967, Lyndon Baines Johnson Library, Austin, Texas. See also Drew Pearson and Jack Anderson, "Christmas at the White House: Joy Is Mingled with Sadness As Johnsons Near the End of a Long Stay in Washington," *The Washington Post*, December 29, 1968. See also Claudia T. Johnson, *Lady Bird Johnson: A White House Diary* (New York: Holt, Rhinehard and Winston, 1970).

Chapter 14: Molding Tradition

The Florida anecdote was found in Julie Nixon Eisenhower, *Pat Nixon* (New York: Simon and Schuster, 1986), 258; other quotations are from

Julie Nixon Eisenhower, telephone interview with author, January 23, 1991, and Dwight David Eisenhower II, telephone interview with author, January 23, 1991.

For a discussion of the historic interpretation of the White House, see Anne Elizabeth Powell, "President's House," *Historic Preservation*, May–June, 1991), 93.

For an account of Christmas at Vail, see Sheila Rabb Weidenfeld, *First Lady's Lady* (New York: G. P. Putnam's Sons, 1979), 243; see also Sheila Weidenfeld, press release, December 25, 1975, Gerald R. Ford Library, Ann Arbor, Michigan.

Chapter 15: A Dark Christmas

The description of the Carters' social life came from Gretchen Poston, interview with author, Washington, D.C., February 5, 1991. For the comment relating to Christmas at the White House, see Rosalynn Carter, *First Lady from Plains* (Boston: Houghton Mifflin Co., 1984), 314; see also Jimmy Carter, *Keeping Faith* (New York: Bantam Books, 1982), 470.

Chapter 16: Nancy Reagan's Perfect Christmas

Comments relating to Christmas at the Reagan White House came from James S. Rosebush, interview with author, New York, N.Y., January 16, 1991; see also James S. Rosebush, *First Lady, Public Wife* (Lanham, Md.: Madison Books, 1987). For a description of White House desserts, see Marian Burros, "Pastry: Delights at White House," *New York Times*, December 9, 1981, Section III, 1, 6. The story relating to the Iran-Contra affair came from Donnie Radcliffe,

"First Lady, Guiding and Chiding," *The Washington Post*, December 9, 1986, C1; see also Victoria Dawson, "Reagan's Media Events," *The Washington Post*, December 12, 1986, C1, C15.

Chapter 17: At Home with the Bush Family

Quotation from George Bush is from "A Message from the President," *Ladies' Home Journal*, December, 1990, 131. The Harrison quotation came from Albert J. Menendez, *Christmas at the White House* (Philadelphia: The Westminster Press, 1983), 111; for the quotation "a universal holiday of men," see Albert J. Menendez, *The December Dilemma* (Silver Spring, Md.: Americans United for Separation of Church and State, 1988), 17. The Henry Adams quotation is from Gore Vidal, *Matters of Fact and Fiction* (New York: Random House, 1977), 172. A different version of the quotation is found in Arthur Schlesinger, Jr., *Crisis of the Old Order*, 354.

Afterword: Symbols of an American Christmas

The Rex Scouten quotation is from Anne Elizabeth Powell, "President's House," *Historic Preservation*, May-June, 1991, 96. For a description of *Lynch v. Donnelly*, see Albert J. Menendez, *The December Dilemma* (Silver Spring, Md.: Americans United for Separation of Church and State, 1988), 33; also see Kelly quotation, 34.

Additional References

In addition to sources appearing in these notes, a wide range of other works relates to the history and folklore of Christmas: Tristram P. Coffin, *Book of Christmas Folklore* (New York: Seabury Press, 1973); Maymie R. Krythe, *All About Christmas* (New York: Harper and Brothers, 1954); Gerald Del Re and Patricia De Re, *The Christmas Almanac* (Garden City, N. Y.: Doubleday and Co., 1979); William DeLoss Love, *Fast and Thanksgiving Days* (Boston: Houghton, Mifflin and Co., 1895); Jessie Wood, ed., *The Time-Life Book of Christmas* (New York: Prentice Hall Press, 1987); and Irena Chalmers, *The Great American Christmas Almanac* (New York: Viking Penguin, 1988). Recipes of Christmas dishes served in the White House have been widely published in magazines and in several White House cookbooks and were not included here. The best collection of updated historic recipes is probably from Eisenhower's chef, François Rysavy, *Treasury of White House Cooking* (New York: G. P. Putnam's Sons, 1962).

Anecdotal material was found also in a variety of White House social histories and books on civility, housekeeping, manners, and protocol at the White House, including Laura C. Holloway, *Ladies of the White House* (Philadelphia: Bradley and Co., 1881); deB Randolph Kelm, *Hand-book of Official and Social Etiquette and Public Ceremonies at Washington* (Washington, D.C.: deB. Randolph Kelm, 1884, found in the collection of the Historical Society of Washington, D. C.); Lillian Rogers Parks, *My Thirty Years Backstairs at the White House* (New York: Fleet Publishing Corporation, 1961); Ben Perley Poore, *Perley's Reminiscences of Sixty Years in the National Metropolis*. vols. 1 and 2 (Philadelphia: Hubbard Brothers, 1886); Ellen Maury Slayden, *Washington Wife: Journal of Ellen Maury Slayden from 1897–1919* (New York: Harper and Row, 1962); Mircea Vasiliu, *The Pleasure is Mine* (New York: Harper and Brothers, 1955); J. B. West, *Upstairs at the White House* (New York: Coward, McCann and Geoghegan, 1973); Anne Hollingsworth Wharton, *Social Life in the Early Republic* (Philadelphia: J. B. Lippincott and Co., 1903); and Mary J. Windle, *Life in Washington* (Philadelphia: J. B. Lippincott and Co., 1859).

General works that contributed to this study include Daniel J. Boorstein, *The Americans: The Colonial Experience* (New York: Random House, 1958), *The Americans: The National Experience* (New York: Random House, 1965), and *The Americans: The Democratic Experience* (New York: Random House, 1973). For a history of changes in the calendar relating to Christmas and New Year's, see William Douglas, *The American Book of Days* (New York: H.W. Wilson Co., 1948). Also consulted were Karen Halttunen, *Confidence Men and Painted Ladies: A Study of Middle-class Culture in America, 1830–1870* (New Haven: Yale University Press, 1982); Richard Hofstadter, *Anti-intellectualism in American Life* (New York: Alfred A. Knopf, 1970); and G. M. Trevelyan, *English Social History* (London: Longmans, Green and Co., 1943).

Photography Credits

The author is grateful to the following organizations and inidividuals for permission to reproduce their copyrighted photographs and artwork.

Index